ORIGAMI

TEACH YOURSELF BOOKS

ORIGAMI

Robert Harbin

TEACH YOURSELF BOOKS

Hodder and Stoughton

To Neal Elias and Fred Rohm

First printed 1968
This revised edition 1980
Eighth impression 1990

ISBN 0 340 25822 5

Printed and bound in Great Britain for
Hodder and Stoughton Educational,
a division of Hodder and Stoughton Ltd,
Mill Road, Dunton Green, Sevenoaks, Kent,
by Richard Clay Ltd, Bungay, Suffolk

This volume is available in the USA from Random House, Inc.,
201 East 50th Street, New York NY 10022

Preface

Writing a book, whatever the subject, is always a laborious task for me. But writing this addition to the Teach Yourself series has been a real pleasure, because I am anxious to introduce as many as possible to the world of origami, which has given me so much enjoyment.

The main task has been to design the illustrations, because without them there could not be a book. Diagrams take a long time to prepare because, fold by fold, the three-dimensional paper model must be reduced to a two-dimensional drawing on a flat sheet of paper. And the drawing must be clear and accurate if the student is to understand how to produce the finished model from it.

It could be argued, I suppose, that origami has an end product that is not worth keeping. Nothing could be further from the truth. At the time of writing, I have a delightful collection of the world's best paper folds, carefully stored in transparent envelopes, which are in turn mounted on a sheet of black board. This way, they are ready to be produced and shown quickly—and they *are* produced and shown, at the slightest provocation!

If this art form captures you, as it has certainly captured me and many others, you will discover that it brings with it a new dimension in enjoyment, which is infinite in its variety and unrivalled in its capacity to make you relax and forget everything else.

Robert Harbin

Contents

A Short History
of Origami

'Origami' is a Japanese word which simply means 'paper-folding' and it
was adopted first in English and then in other languages in recognition
of the long tradition of the Japanese people for folding paper.

The Chinese invented paper, probably before the birth of Christ, and
we can only guess that they were the first to fold paper. But we do know
that by the twelfth century A.D. paper was used in Japan for folding
ceremonial wrappers ('tsutsumi') for storage of household goods, such
as herbs, and for gifts, especially gifts of flowers, where each kind of
flower had its special wrapper. The present-day Japanese custom of
attaching to gifts small tokens of folded paper called 'noshi' is a relic of
this ceremonial paper-folding and there remain some other survivals.

Apart from occasional far-from-clear references to paper animals,
birds and flowers, the earliest informative records we have of recrea-
tional, as opposed to ceremonial, paper-folding are two Japanese books
the *Senbazuru Orikata* and the *Chushingura Orikata* both dating from
1797. The first describes how to fold connected groups and chains of
paper cranes (very similar to the classic flapping bird on page 88) and
the second shows how to fold a series of characters from a popular play.
These paper dolls resemble somewhat Robert Harbin's Japanese Lady
and Gentleman on pages 156 to 160. The folding in these two books is
much more advanced than the simple folds familiar to children round
the world and it presupposes a long tradition of paper-folding in Japan
before 1800.

The little paper dolls appear again in the *Kan no mado*, a manuscript
encyclopaedia believed to date from the middle of the nineteenth
century. This contains several ceremonial folds and also some elaborately
folded animals and insects which use extensive cutting: something which
would not be acceptable today.

As modern creative origami avoids cutting it does not derive directly from the tradition of the *Kan no mado* and it is the flapping bird itself which lies at the heart of the modern development of the art. This remarkable folded toy was brought to Europe by Japanese stage magicians about 1870 and was quickly absorbed into the small European repertoire of children's folds. The Spanish philosopher Miguel de Unamuno (1864–1936) took a delight in childish things including paper-folding and by manipulating the bird base he created a series of somewhat angular birds and animals which nevertheless greatly extended the possibilities of paper-folding. His most significant discovery was the sideways twist of the flaps of the bird base which is also used in Yoshizawa's pigeon (page 91). A small group of followers of Unanumo came into being and the Praying Moor (page 97) is an example of their work. The Spanish tradition spread to South America and culminated in the vast analytical work of Dr. Solorzano Sagredo and the delicately creative work of his pupil, the late Ligia Montoya of Argentina, two of whose simpler models are the Tropical Birds on pages 127 to 131.

In Japan, Isao Honda made collections of traditional and modern origami and new books began to appear, notably those by Michio Uchiyama and his son Kosho Uchiyama. Then, quite independently of Unanumo, Akira Yoshizawa made similar discoveries about the possibilities of the bird base. Some of his work was published by Isao Honda in 1944. After the Second World War, Yoshizawa began to publish his own books and articles and Japanese paper-folding entered a new period of creativity. Akira Yoshizawa's ingenuity is matched by his incomparable skill in bringing his models to life and he continues to dominate the art in Japan.

Before the war, paper-folding in English-speaking countries had been limited to the traditional children's folds, but in the 1950s it began to develop through the efforts of three people: Gershon Legman and Lillian Oppenheimer of the United States and Robert Harbin of Britain. Curiously none of them claimed to be a creative folder. Gershon Legman compiled a bibliography and also established contacts with both Akira Yoshizawa and Ligia Montoya. Lillian Oppenheimer publicised origami, put folders in touch with one another and made many books available including some in Spanish and Japanese. Robert Harbin demonstrated paper-folding on television for the first time in 1955, and in 1956 he published his excellent book *Paper Magic* which summarised the art and for a time became the standard manual in English.

The work of these three people brought together for the first time many people who had been folding paper for their own amusement in isolation and the newly available books inspired a generation of creative folders, especially in America where Fred Rohm, Neal Elias, Robert Neale, George Rhoads and Jack Skillman devised new techniques and basic folds which opened up possibilities for paper-folding undreamed of even in Japan. For a time the bird base and its related folds, the fish base and frog base remained the foundations for folding but they were soon joined by more complex versions including multiple and 'blinzed' bird and frog bases. Before long entirely new ideas emerged including the 'box-folding' of Dr. Emanuel Mooser of Switzerland and 'box-pleating' developed especially by Neal Elias.

Despite the influence of Robert Harbin, paper-folding in Britain lagged behind until the British Origami Society was formed in 1967 from a group of folders whom Lillian Oppenheimer had put in touch with each other. The Society developed slowly but its membership grew following the original publication of *Teach Yourself Origami* in 1968. Since then the Society's magazine *British Origami* has become one of the world's leading journals on the subject.

In the 1970s, just when some began to think that the limits of folding had been reached, members of the British Origami Society broke new ground and produced a large number of greatly varied models of remarkable ingenuity, widely differing in style, sometimes mechanical, sometimes artistic. The classic bird and frog bases were now abandoned by creative folders and new, specialised bases were developed uniquely appropriate for the model to be folded.

The new Western techniques have now been taken back to Japan and a new generation of Japanese folders has started to combine the mechanical virtuosity of the West with the delicate artistry of the East.

The happiest thing about paper-folding is that it has grown as a truly international movement and groups in North and South America, Britain, France, Spain, Italy, Japan and many other countries are in regular touch with each other. New discoveries are shared and exhibitions are held to which contributions are sent from all over the world. It was Robert Harbin's heartfelt wish that his beloved origami should ever continue to bring friendship to the people of every land, and by sharing in that hope paper-folders will best honour his memory.

David Lister

3

Information on supplies and membership of the British Origami Society can be obtained from:

The Secretary
Origami Society
12 Thorn Road
Bramhall
Stockport
CHESHIRE SK7 1BQ

The British Origami Society has published a series of booklets of very varied interests including the advanced work of some of the world's leading creative folders. The Society also has available for members a wide selection of books in English and other languages, including Japanese. Write to The Secretary for information.

The Essentials of Origami

As you have decided to learn origami, you will be anxious to start work on the models in this book. First, though, the following essential instructions must be read carefully.

Most beginners are not able to follow diagrams and instructions easily and successfully, however carefully they may have been planned. As a rule, origami illustrators try to cram into each page as much information as possible. This practice is welcomed by the enthusiast and the expert, because it means that the book will be able to explain a large number of models. Unfortunately, though, a page filled with diagrams completely bewilders most beginners.

I have borne this in mind while preparing this book, and you will see that the earlier pages have been designed with no more than two or three diagrams on each page. All the diagrams are clearly drawn, and contain instructions and symbols to give you all possible help, and to explain the mainly standard models which bring you in touch with most of the Basic Folds.

A Basic Fold is a fold from which many models can be made. There are many Basic Folds, both ancient and modern, but this book will introduce you to just enough to give you a good groundwork on which to begin.

Look at the first fold illustrated in the book, and notice how the instructions are placed on the parts to be folded: FOLD THIS SIDE DOWN, and then TO HERE, and so on. The instructions are made to work for you. Later in the book, the instructions are placed next to the diagrams, and not on them, because it is assumed that by then you will have become familiar with the different processes.

Always fold carefully, accurately and neatly. If you fold carelessly, the result will be disastrous.

Study each diagram showing the complete folded model, and only then, place your origami paper in front of you and make your first fold.

When you make a fold, always crease the paper firmly with the back of your thumbnail. Good creases make folding easy, and are an invaluable guide later in the model, when you are making a series of folds.

Pre-creasing is an important feature. Consider, for example, the Japanese Lady (page 15). This model was sent to Samuel Randlett, who immediately used the idea to produce his fine Fish (page 161). Notice how he pre-creases the paper he uses so that everything folds into place at the right moment.

Before you make a Reverse Fold, pre-crease the paper by folding the whole thickness before opening the paper and making the fold (see Reverse Folds).

Notice how paper coloured on one side is used to get the maximum effect for each model. The subject of paper is an important one. Origami paper should be strong, thin and suitably coloured. But if you cannot find special origami paper, almost any paper may be used.

If you are instructed to use a square of paper, make sure that it really is square, and that a rectangle is a true rectangle. Most of the models in this book are based on squares of paper, but there is no regular rule about this, as all shapes of paper can be used, according to the model's needs. See, for example, the Ornithonimus (page 165) and Aladdin's Lamp (page 168).

Origami is not a simple art. To the expert, it is a challenge to the eye, the brain and the fingers—a wonderful mental and physical therapy.

When you fold one of the decorations explained in this book, you will find that by altering this or that fold you can invent endless shapes. In fact, you can improvise for hours.

When you have mastered the Basic Folds, you will then be equipped to produce figures and shapes of your own invention. Have something in mind, and then consider the best Base from which to start. You will notice that there are three different ways in which to make a penguin. The penguin seems to be a favourite subject, and almost every folder has a go at it.

Watch out for terms like Squash Fold. It is so named because you do just that—squash the part indicated so that the sides bulge and it flattens, in most cases symmetrically.

Study the Petal Folds, the Rabbit's Ears and the various Bases, and try to remember what they are. If you get stuck, have a look at the Contents and refer to the pages concerned.

You will notice that certain procedures are used over and over again. You will soon get used to these and be able to carry them out automatically.

When you have folded everything in the first half of the book, you will find that more and more diagrams begin to appear on each page, and that the symbols begin to play a bigger part than the instructions. Decoration 2 (page 151) has been included as an exercise so try to make this up using the symbols only.

Start at the beginning of the book and work your way through. Do not attempt anything too difficult to start with, because this can only end in disappointment.

For the rehabilitation of damaged hands there is nothing like origami for making reluctant fingers come back to life.

Finally—take it slowly; fold carefully, neatly and accurately. And START AT THE BEGINNING!

A Note on Symbols

The symbols used in this book are based on Akira Yoshizawa's code of lines and arrows. Symbols will become second nature to you when folding as they are easy to acquire.

The moment you see a line of dashes, you know that the paper must be Valley Folded along that line. When you see a line of dashes and dots, you recognise the sign for a Mountain Fold. To make a Mountain Fold, you naturally turn the paper upside down and make a Valley Fold.

Arrows show the directions in which you must fold: left, right, up, down, in front, behind and into.

You will notice one arrow which shows that a drawing has been enlarged for clarity. Another arrow indicates that a model must be opened out (see Samuel Randlett's Fish, page 161). My own little black arrow indicates that you must sink, press, squeeze or push in at certain points.

The symbols are in fact self-explanatory. They are simple common sense, and can be learnt in about ten minutes.

Try to use the symbols only and ignore explanations. This will help you when you come to read Japanese origami books.

INTERNATIONAL ORIGAMI SYMBOLS

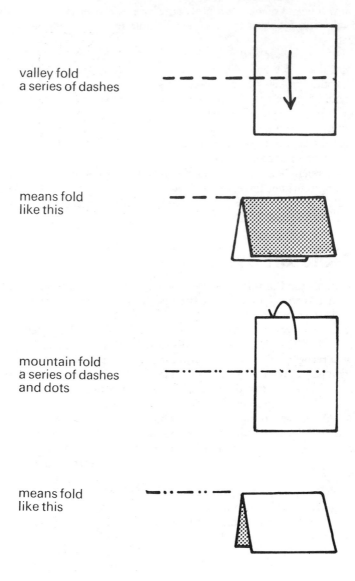

valley fold
a series of dashes

means fold
like this

mountain fold
a series of dashes
and dots

means fold
like this

if a drawing
was marked
with these symbols

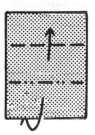

the result
should be
this

when a drawing
is followed by
this little looped
arrow

turn the
model over
so

this black arrow

means push in

thin lines mean creases

this symbol

means

fold over and over

MAKE THIS WATER BOMB BASE AND PRELIMINARY FOLD

if a drawing is
marked like this

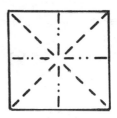

you make this
water bomb base

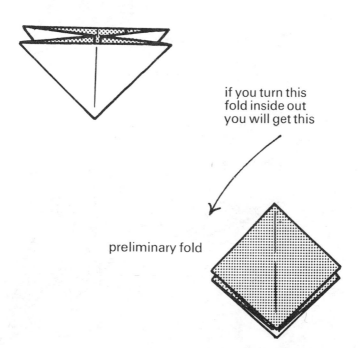

if you turn this
fold inside out
you will get this

preliminary fold

reverse fold 1

crease

note how paper is
marked. crease
along the mark.
now reverse fold
as shown

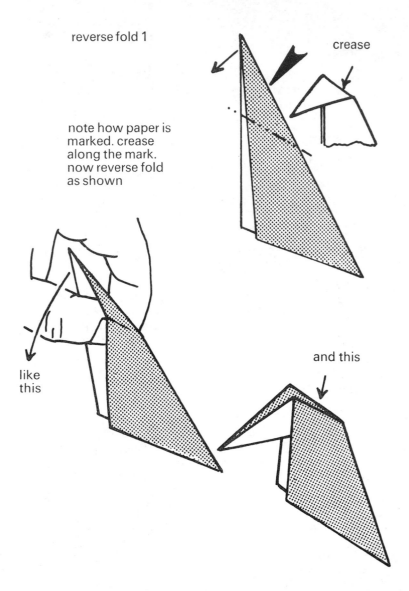

like
this

and this

reverse fold 2

crease

note how paper is
marked. crease
along the mark.
now reverse fold
as shown

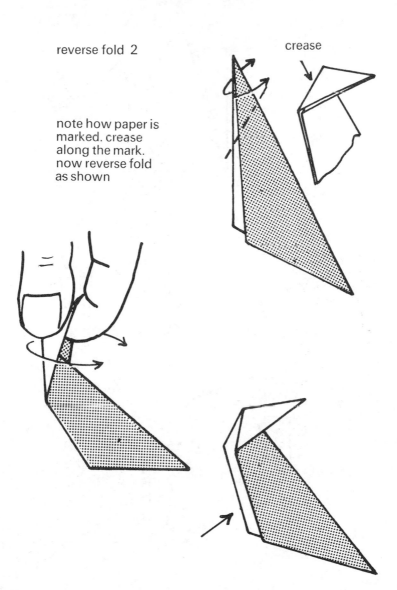

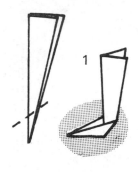

1

how to fold feet.
(birds, animals, people.)
1. reverse fold 2
2. reverse fold 1
3. two reverse folds

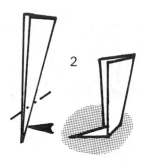

2

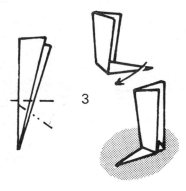

3

HOW TO MAKE A BIRD'S HEAD

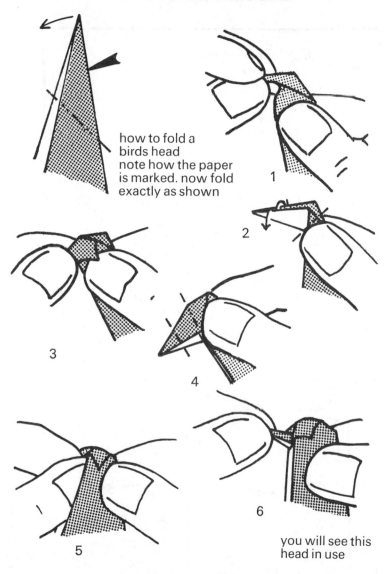

how to fold a
birds head
note how the paper
is marked. now fold
exactly as shown

1

2

3

4

5

6

you will see this
head in use

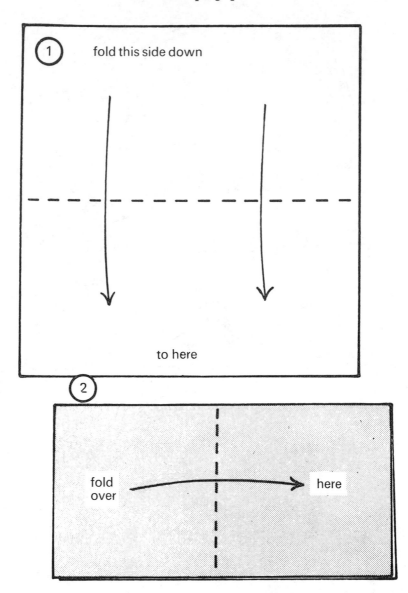

1 fold this side down

to here

2 fold over → here

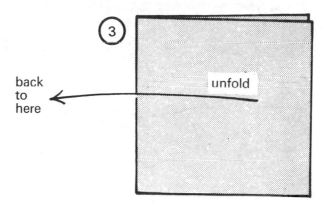

back
to
here

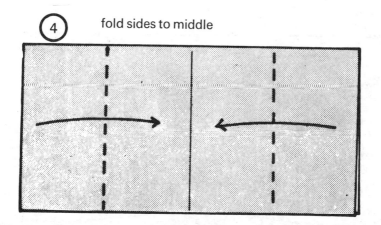

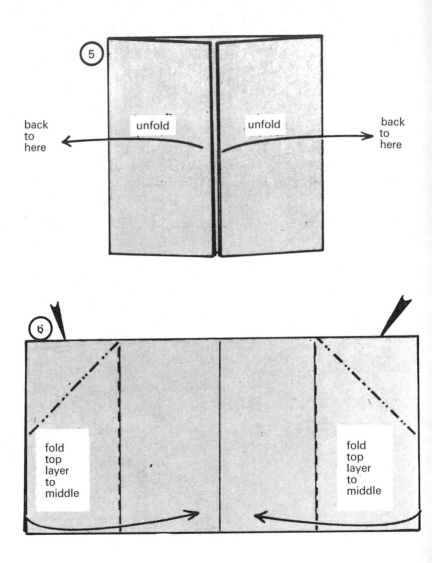

⑤ back to here ← unfold   unfold → back to here

⑥ fold top layer to middle   fold top layer to middle

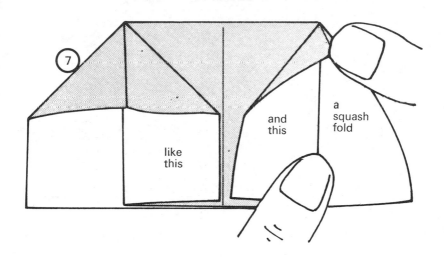

like
this

and
this

a
squash
fold

now draw doors and windows

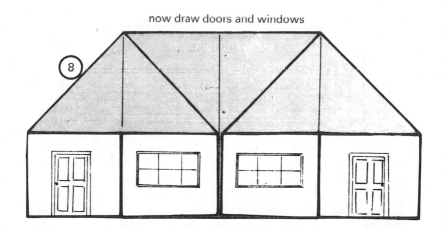

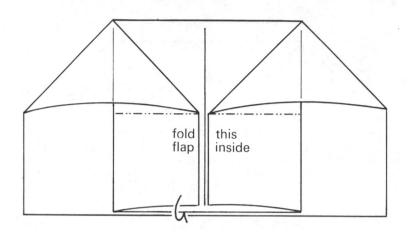

fold | this
flap | inside

now –
turn the
model over

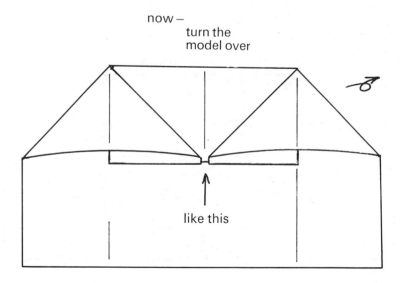

like this

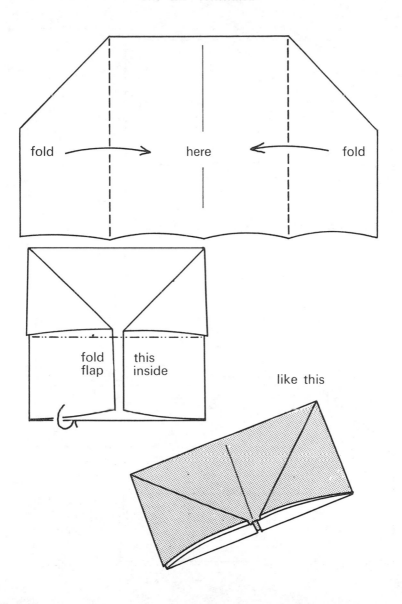

fold ——————→ here ←—————— fold

fold
flap

this
inside

like this

BOAT *Use a square of paper*

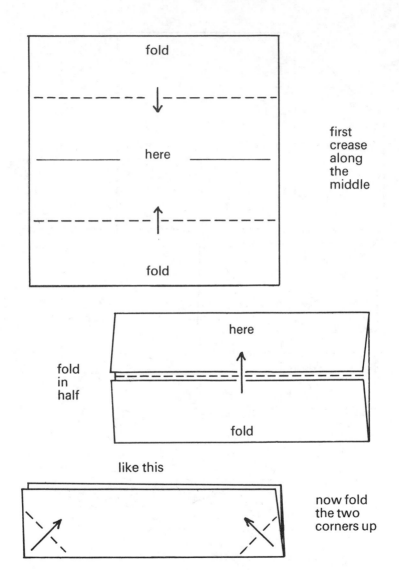

fold

↓

here

fold

↑

first
crease
along
the
middle

here

↑

fold in half

fold

like this

now fold
the two
corners up

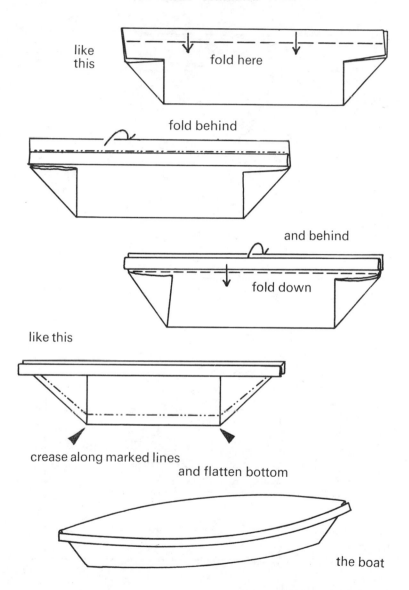

like
this
fold here

fold behind

and behind

fold down

like this

crease along marked lines
and flatten bottom

the boat

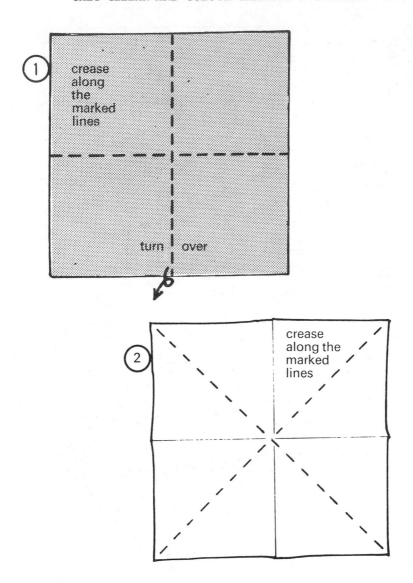

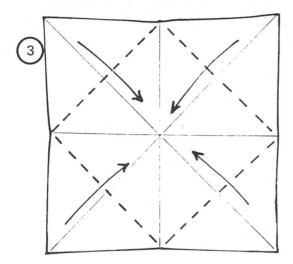

③

now fold the corners in

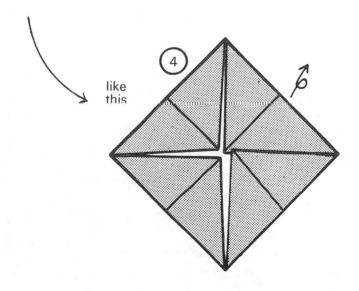

④

like this

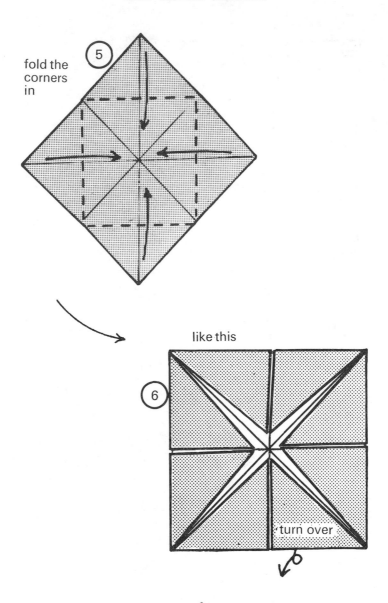

5 fold the corners in

like this

6 turn over

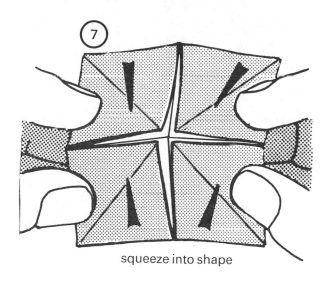

squeeze into shape

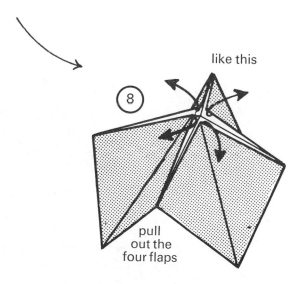

like this

pull
out the
four flaps

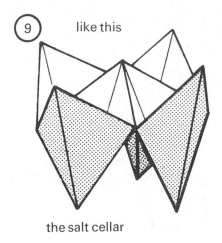

⑨ like this

the salt cellar

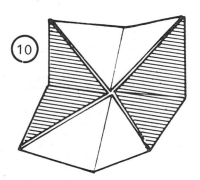

⑩ this is the salt cellar
upside down. colour
the areas shown

to make
the colour
changer

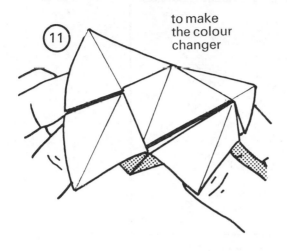

and this
shows how you
make it work

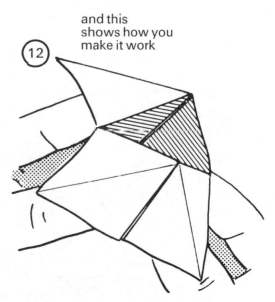

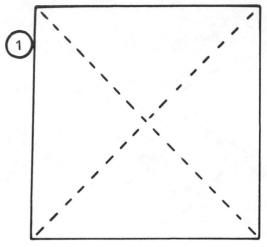

crease along the marked lines

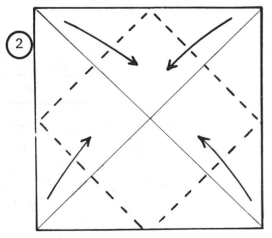

fold the four corners to the centre

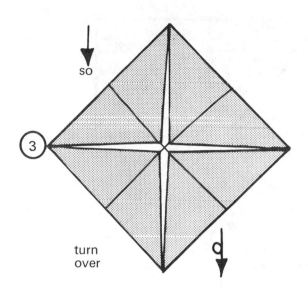

so

③

turn
over

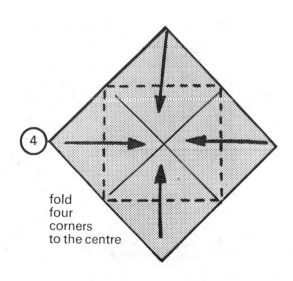

④

fold
four
corners
to the centre

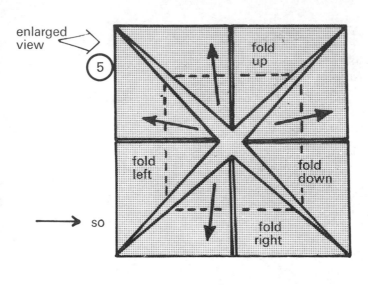

enlarged view

⑤

fold up

fold left

fold down

fold right

so

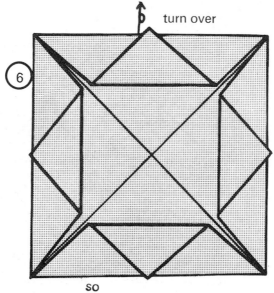

⑥

turn over

so

32

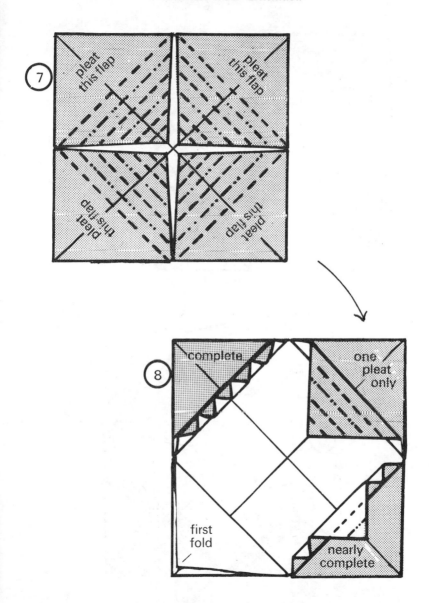

7

pleat this flap

pleat this flap

pleat this flap

pleat this flap

8

complete

one pleat only

first fold

nearly complete

33

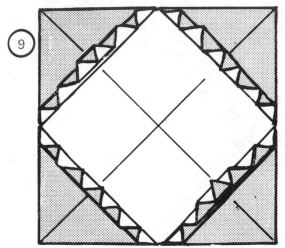

completed pleats

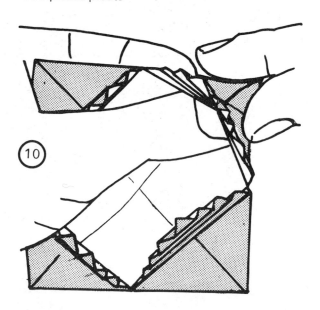

push left thumb into each
corner and press together
on the outside until the
fancy box is completed

so

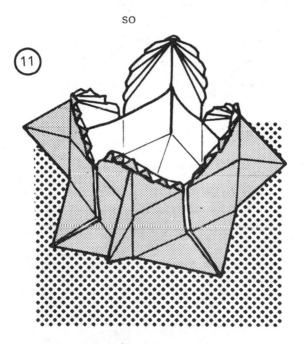

fill the box with sweets

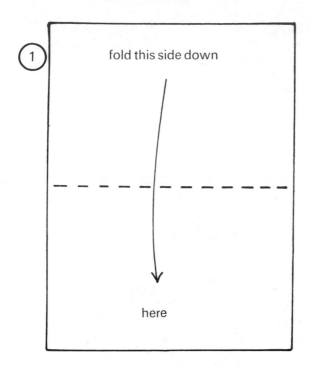

(1) fold this side down

here

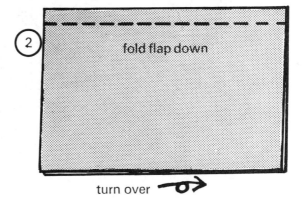

(2) fold flap down

turn over ⟶

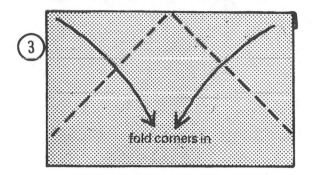

③ fold corners in

like this

④

fold this flap over
twice

37

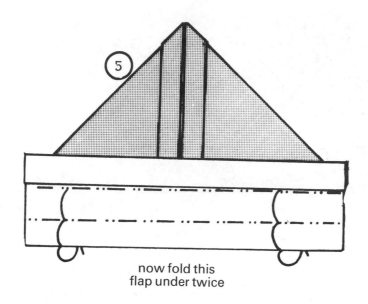

now fold this
flap under twice

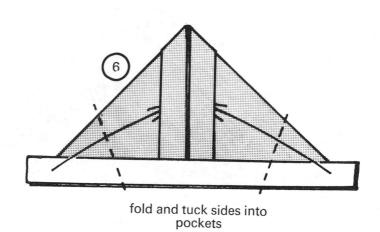

fold and tuck sides into
pockets

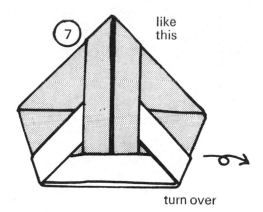

7 like
this

turn over

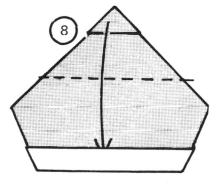

8

fold down top
and tuck into
pocket

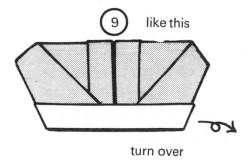

9 like this

turn over

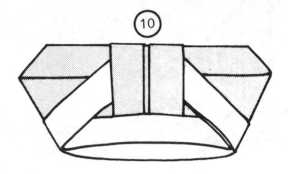

the turban complete

try this with
a sheet of
newspaper

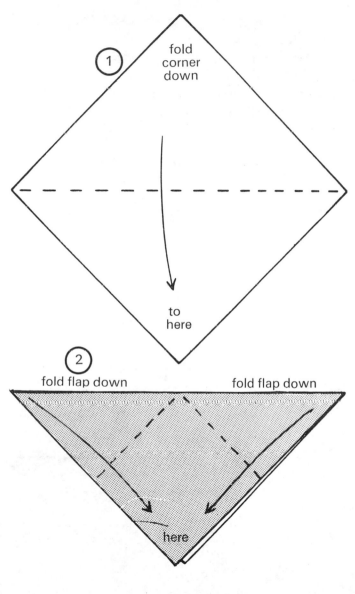

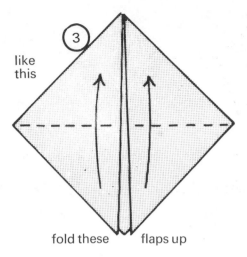

like
this

fold these flaps up

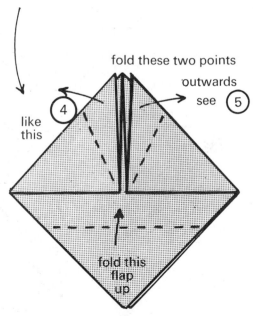

fold these two points

outwards

see ⑤

like
this

fold this
flap
up

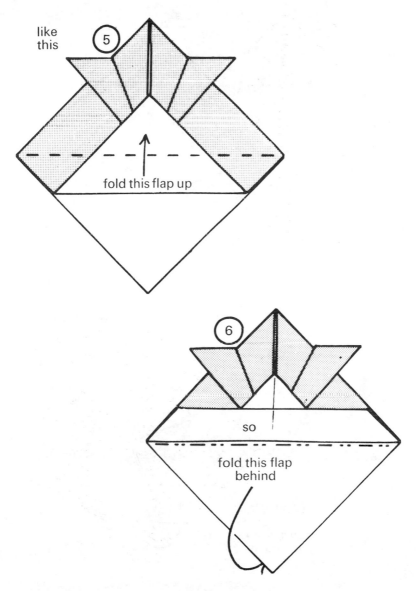

like
this

⑤

fold this flap up

⑥

so

fold this flap
behind

43

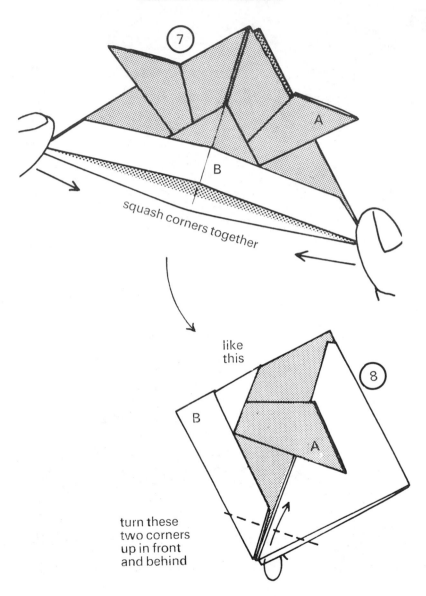

squash corners together

like
this

turn these
two corners
up in front
and behind

44

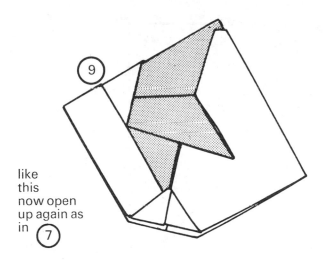

like
this
now open
up again as
in (7)

a piece of paper
20 inches square
will make a hat
to fit your head

like this

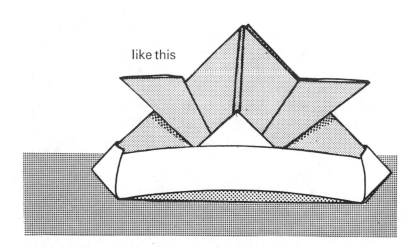

45

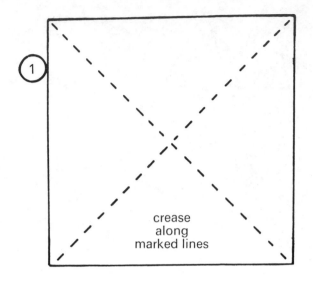

crease
along
marked lines

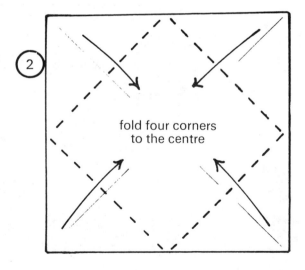

fold four corners
to the centre

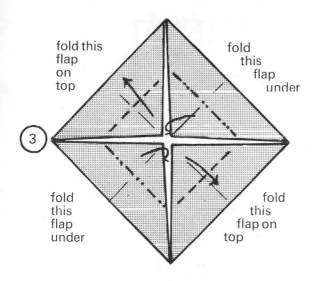

fold this
flap
on
top

fold
this
flap
under

③

fold
this
flap
under

fold
this
flap on
top

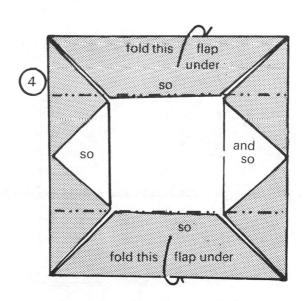

fold this flap under

④

so

so

and
so

so

fold this flap under

47

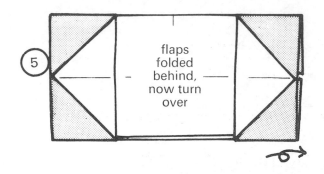

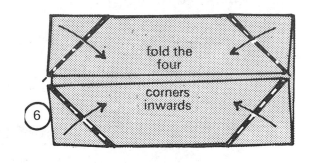

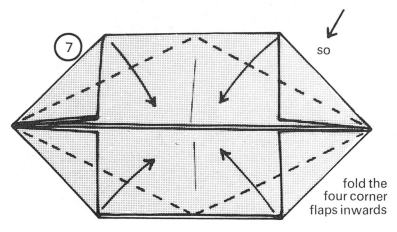

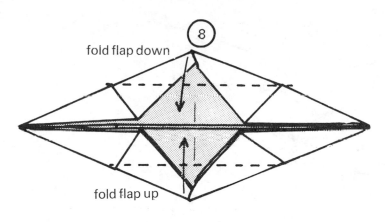

⑧ fold flap down

fold flap up

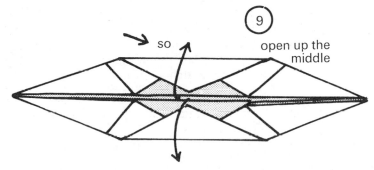

⑨ so   open up the
middle

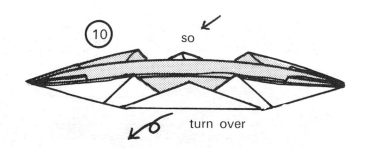

⑩ so

turn over

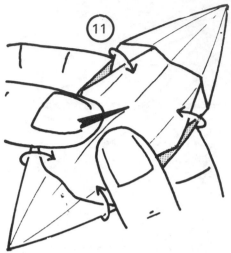

press thumbs in, then
with fingers pull
sides up — and so
turn the boat
inside out — the
result will be
this

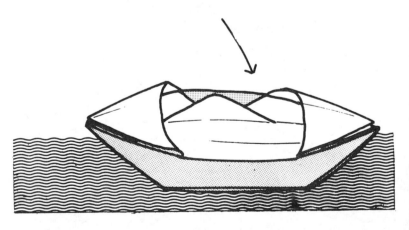

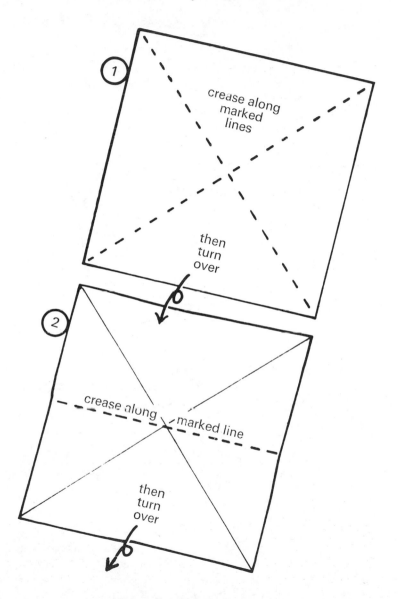

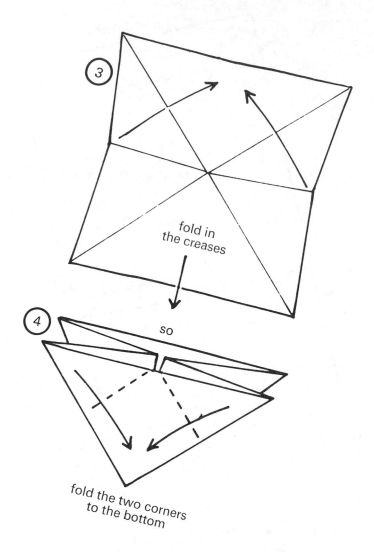

3

fold in
the creases

so

4

fold the two corners
to the bottom

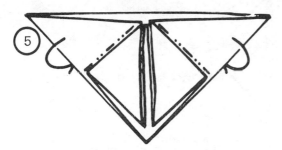

fold the two corners behind

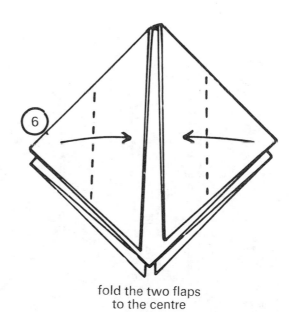

fold the two flaps
to the centre

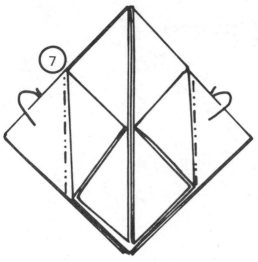

fold the two
flaps behind

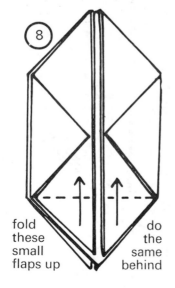

fold
these
small
flaps up

do
the
same
behind

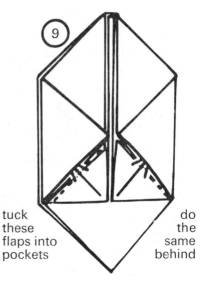

tuck
these
flaps into
pockets

do
the
same
behind

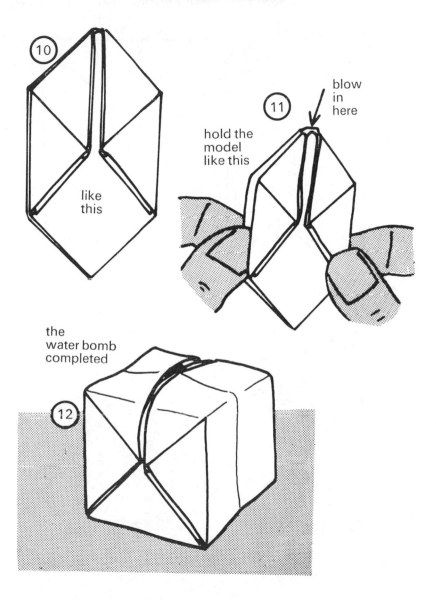

⑩ like this

⑪ hold the
model
like this

blow
in
here

the
water bomb
completed

⑫

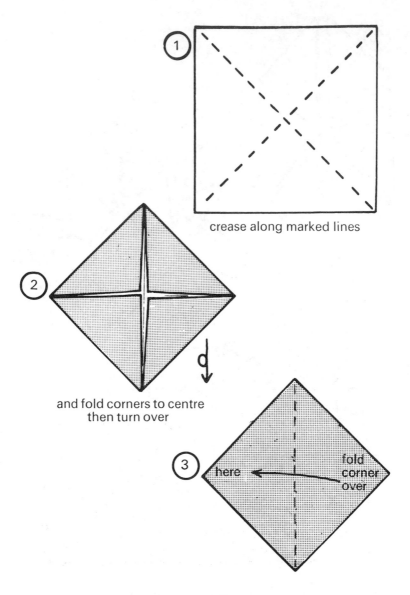

1 crease along marked lines

2 and fold corners to centre
then turn over

3 here fold corner over

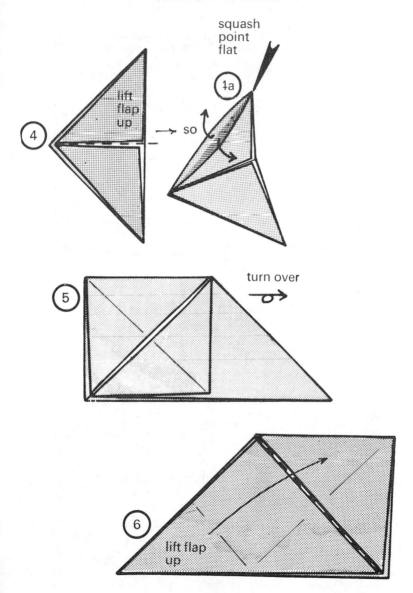

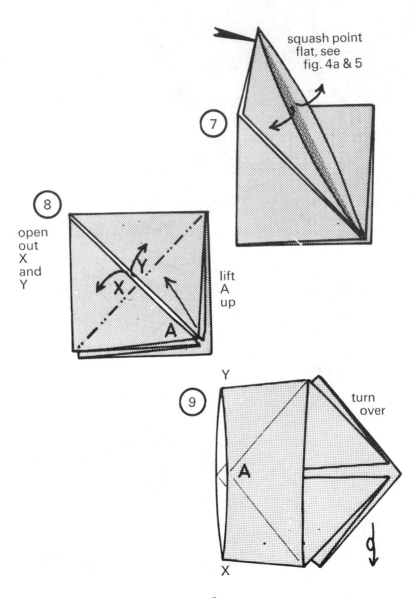

squash point
flat, see
fig. 4a & 5

7

8

open
out
X
and
Y

lift
A
up

9

Y

A

turn
over

X

58

open out X and Y

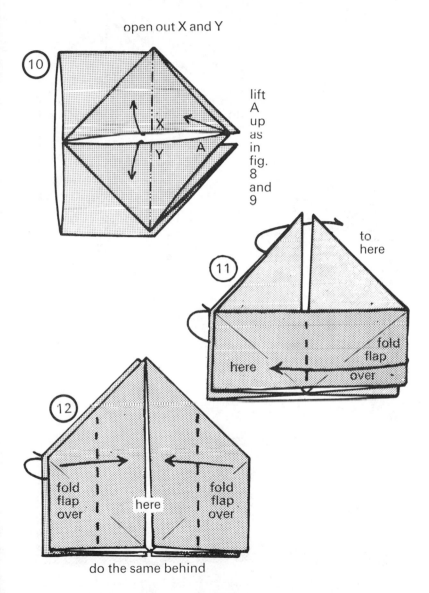

10

lift
A
up
as
in
fig.
8
and
9

11

to
here

fold
flap
over

here

12

fold
flap
over

here

fold
flap
over

do the same behind

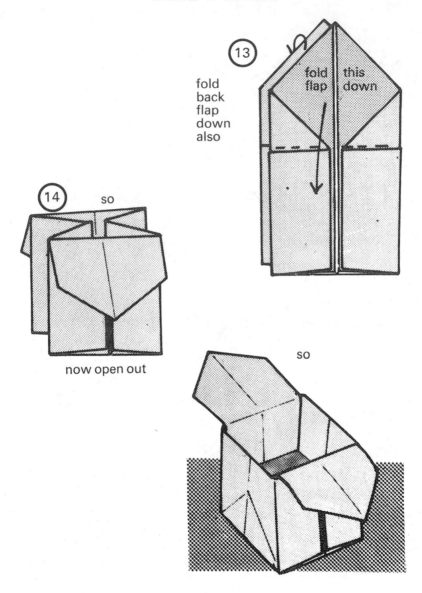

(13)

fold
back
flap
down
also

fold this
flap down

(14)   so

now open out

so

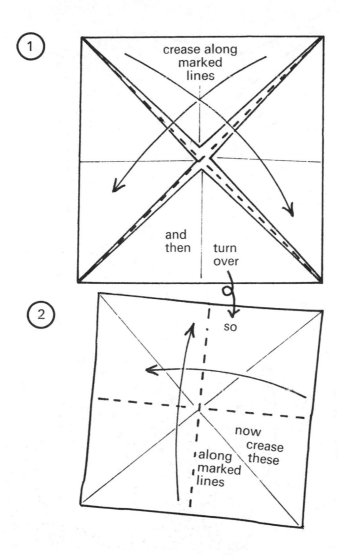

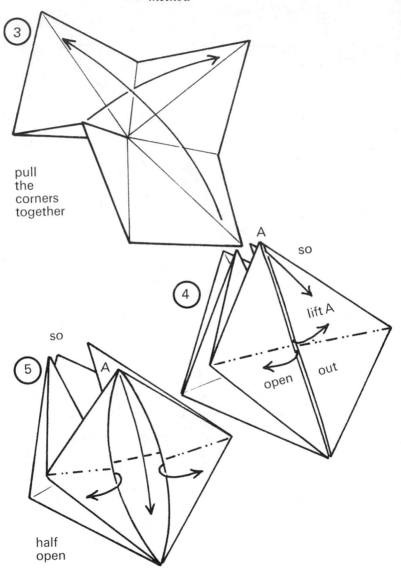

③ pull
the
corners
together

④ A so
lift A
open out

⑤ so
A
half
open

62

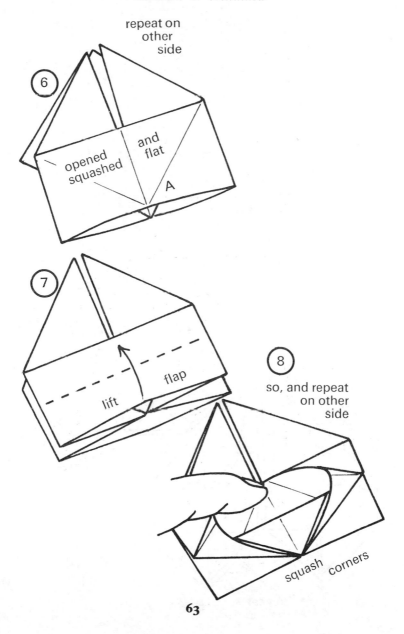

repeat on
other
side

6

opened
squashed

and
flat

A

7

lift

flap

8

so, and repeat
on other
side

squash corners

63

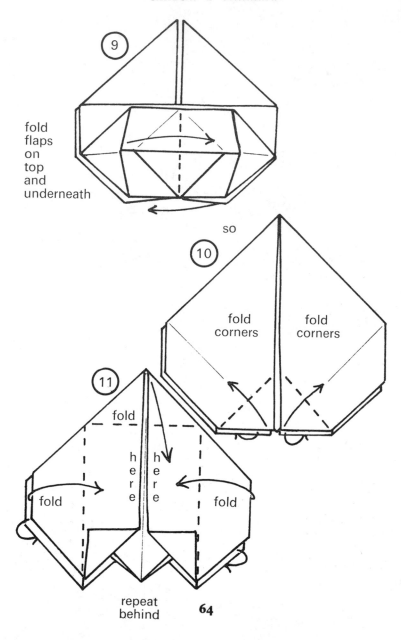

9 fold flaps on top and underneath

so

10 fold corners   fold corners

11 fold

fold here here fold

fold

repeat behind

64

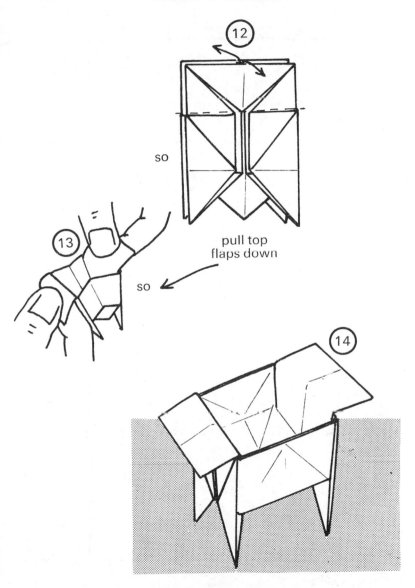

so

pull top
flaps down

so

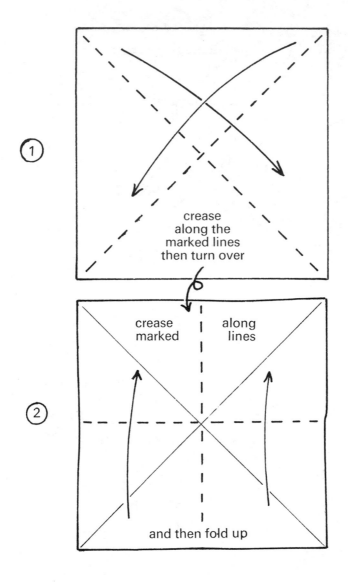

crease
along the
marked lines
then turn over

crease   along
marked   lines

and then fold up

so

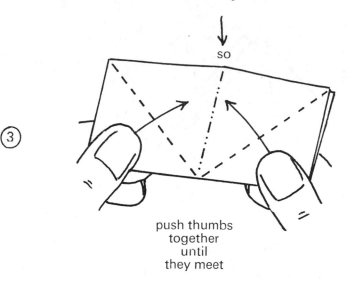

③

push thumbs
together
until
they meet

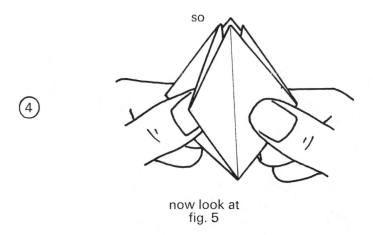

④

so

now look at
fig. 5

67

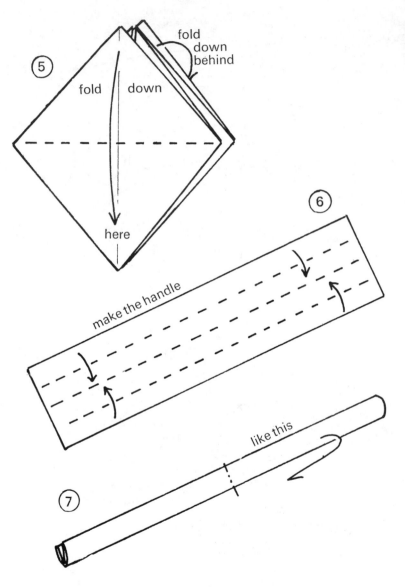

⑤ fold down
fold down behind
here

⑥ make the handle

⑦ like this

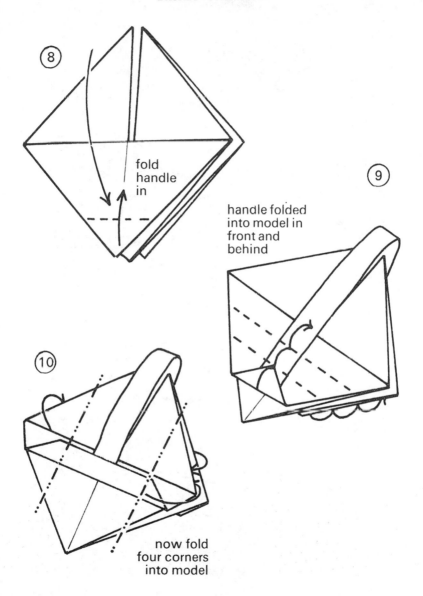

⑧ fold
handle
in

⑨ handle folded
into model in
front and
behind

⑩ now fold
four corners
into model

BASKET *continued*

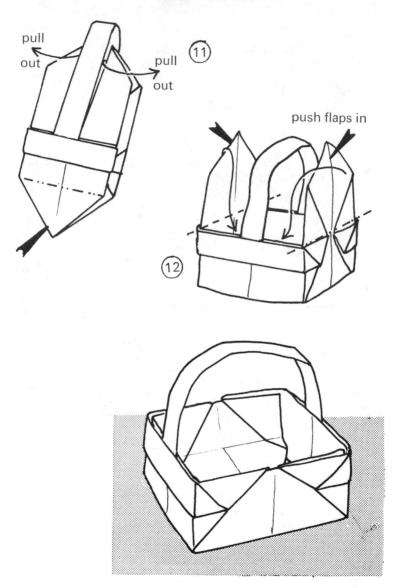

pull
out

pull
out

⑪

push flaps in

⑫

70

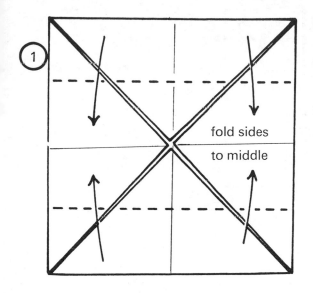

fold sides
to middle

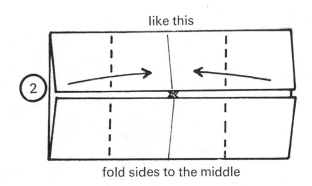

like this

fold sides to the middle

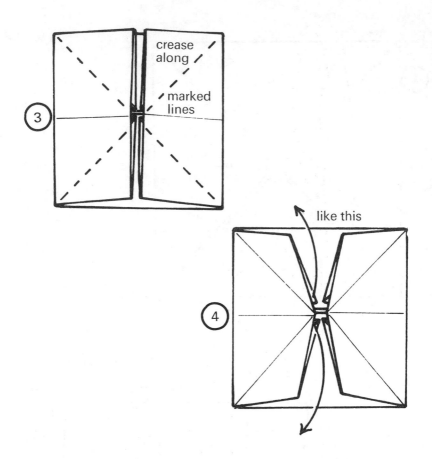

crease
along

marked
lines

like this

now pull out the
two arrowed
points, the creases
will guide you and
they will fall into
place as in fig. 5

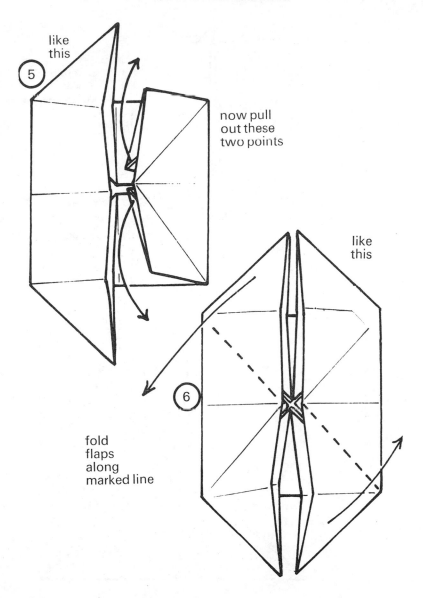

like
this

⑤

now pull
out these
two points

like
this

⑥

fold
flaps
along
marked line

73

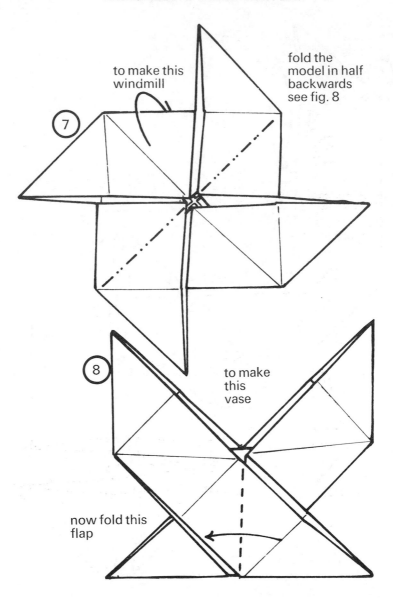

to make this
windmill

fold the
model in half
backwards
see fig. 8

⑦

⑧

to make
this
vase

now fold this
flap

74

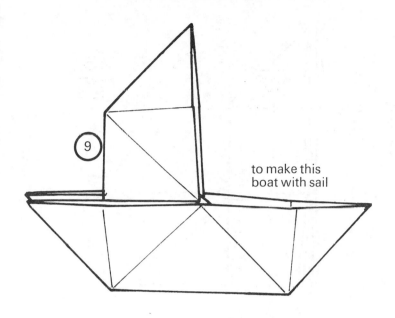

9

to make this
boat with sail

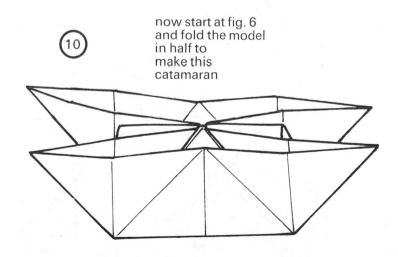

10

now start at fig. 6
and fold the model
in half to
make this
catamaran

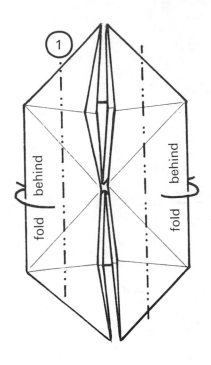

fold behind

fold behind

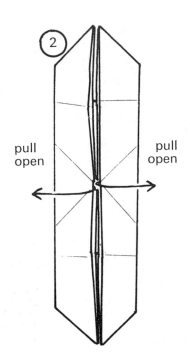

pull open

pull open

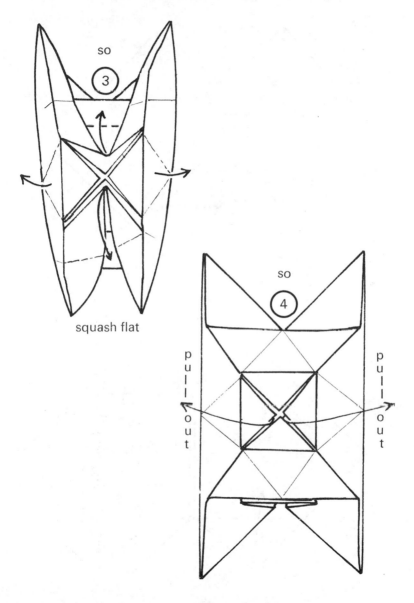

so

③

squash flat

so

④

p
u
l
l
o
u
t

p
u
l
l
o
u
t

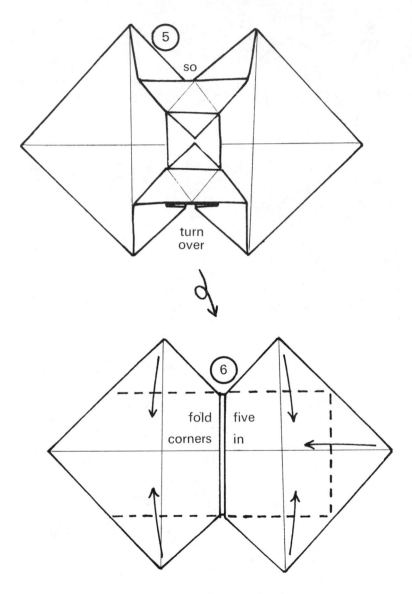

5

so

turn
over

6

fold   five

corners   in

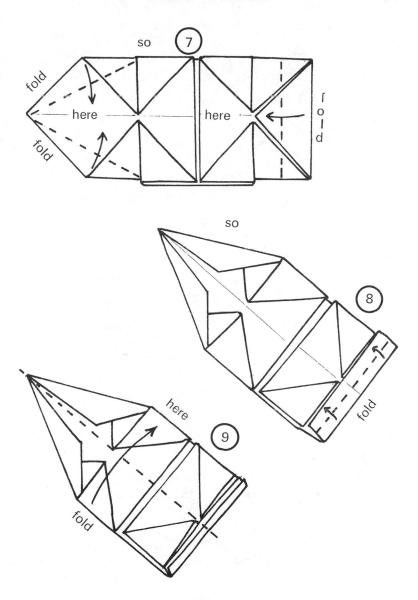

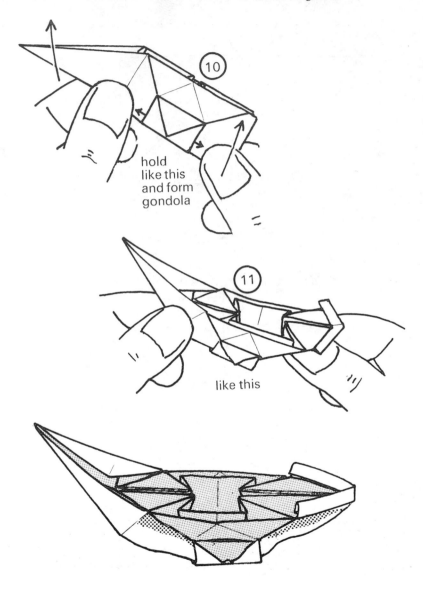

hold
like this
and form
gondola

like this

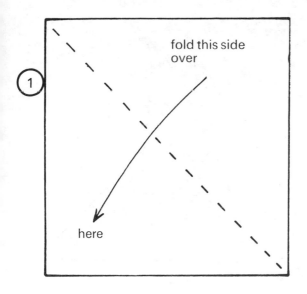

fold this side
over

here

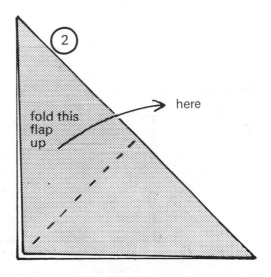

here

fold this
flap
up

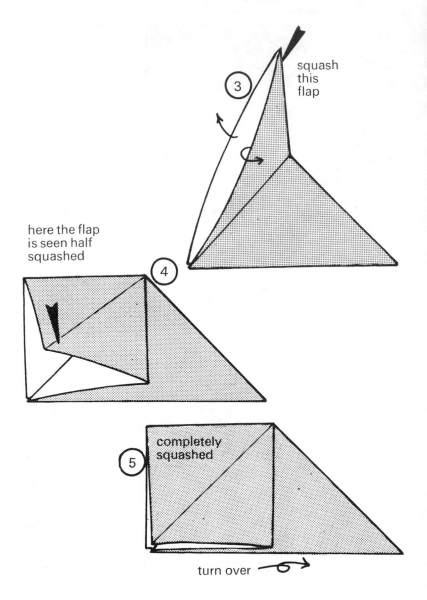

squash
this
flap

③

here the flap
is seen half
squashed

④

⑤ completely
squashed

turn over

82

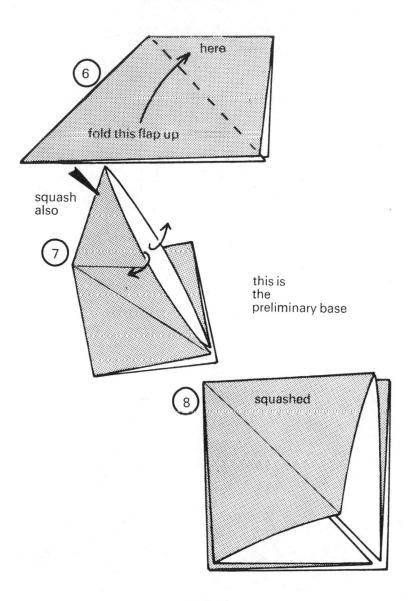

6 here

fold this flap up

squash
also

7 this is
the
preliminary base

8 squashed

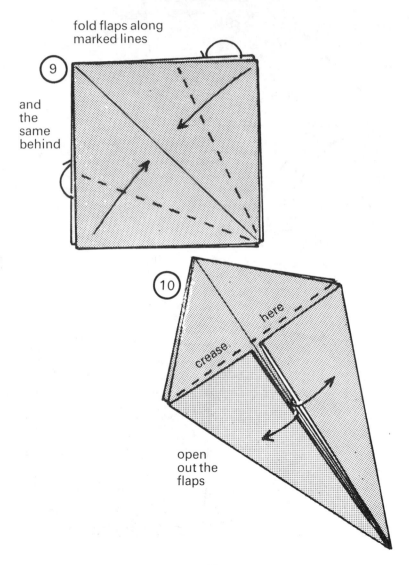

fold flaps along
marked lines

⑨

and
the
same
behind

⑩

crease

here

open
out the
flaps

84

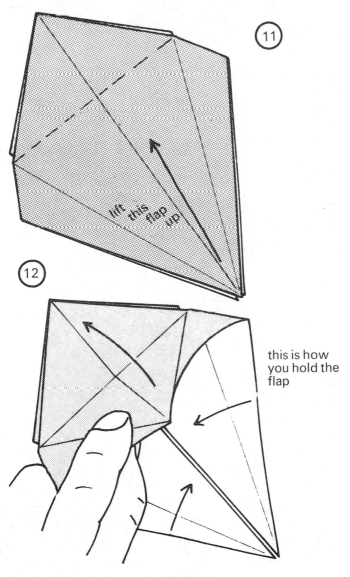

11

lift this flap up

12

this is how
you hold the
flap

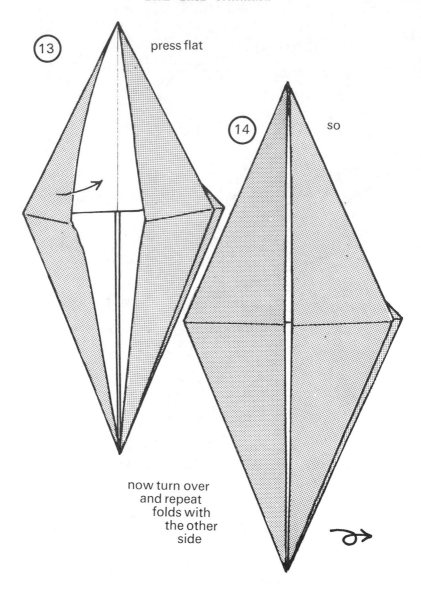

(13) press flat

now turn over
and repeat
folds with
the other
side

(14) so

86

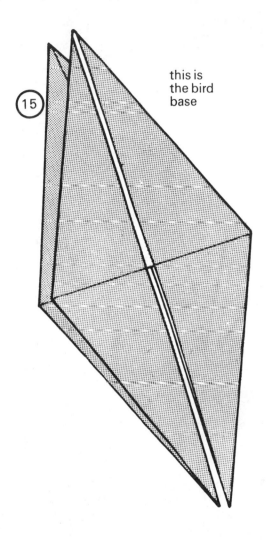

this is
the bird
base

(15)

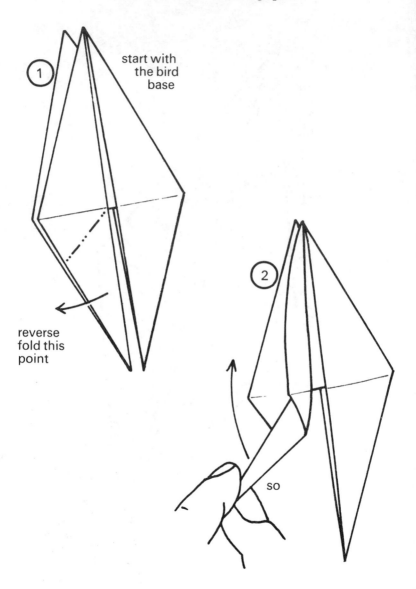

start with
the bird
base

reverse
fold this
point

so

88

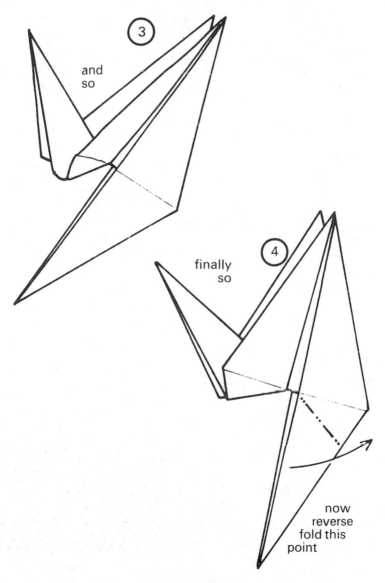

③ and
so

④ finally
so

now
reverse
fold this
point

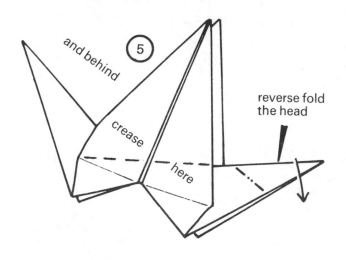

⑤ and behind

crease here

reverse fold the head

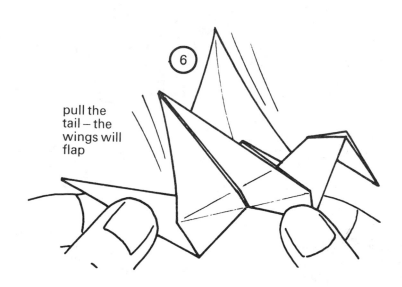

⑥ pull the tail – the wings will flap

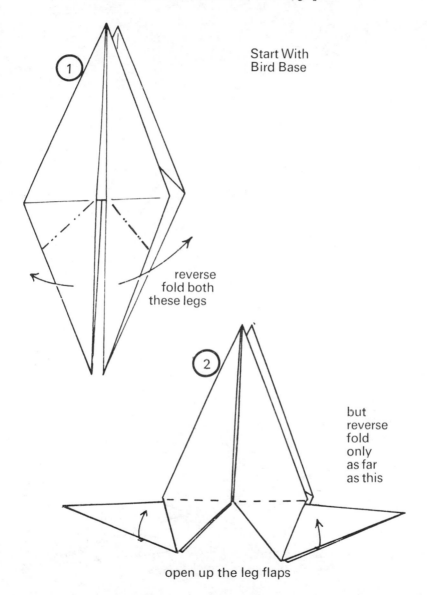

Start With
Bird Base

1

reverse
fold both
these legs

2

but
reverse
fold
only
as far
as this

open up the leg flaps

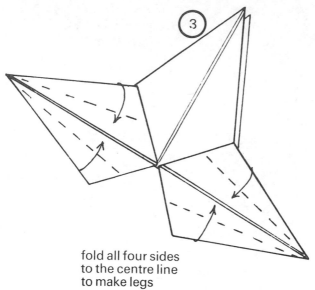

fold all four sides
to the centre line
to make legs

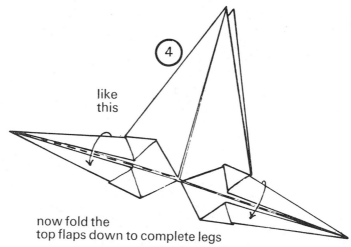

like
this

now fold the
top flaps down to complete legs

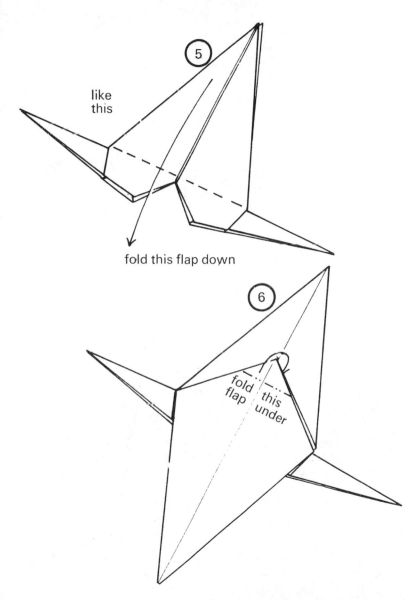

like
this

fold this flap down

fold this
flap under

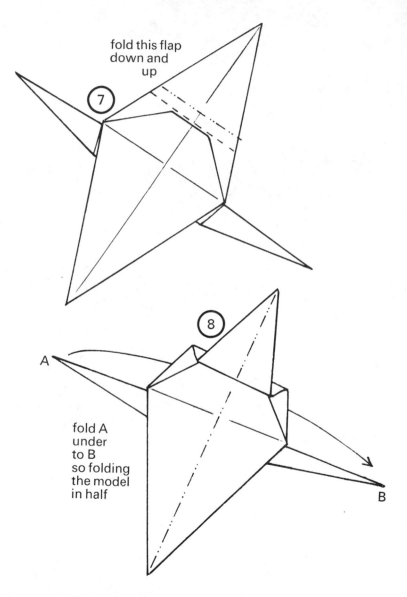

fold this flap
down and
up

⑦

⑧

A

fold A
under
to B
so folding
the model
in half

B

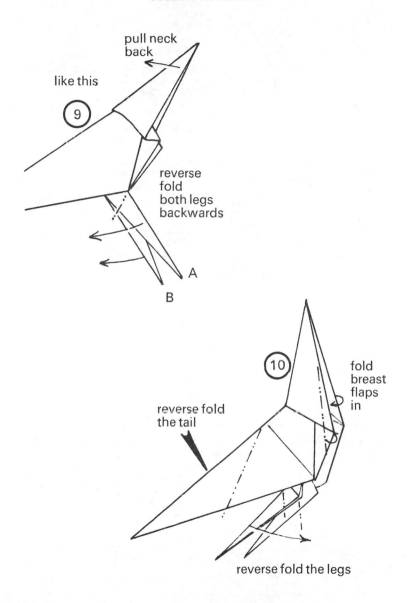

pull neck back

like this

(9)

reverse fold both legs backwards

A

B

(10)

fold breast flaps in

reverse fold the tail

reverse fold the legs

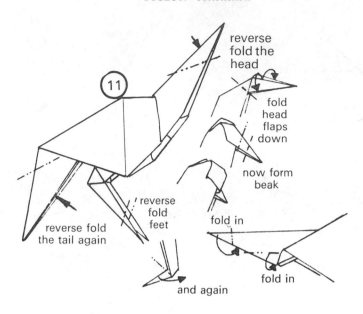

(11)

reverse
fold the
head

fold
head
flaps
down

now form
beak

reverse
fold feet

reverse
fold
feet

reverse fold
the tail again

fold in

fold in

and again

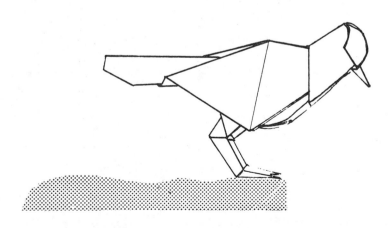

PRAYING MOOR *Spanish Origin. Start with Bird Base*

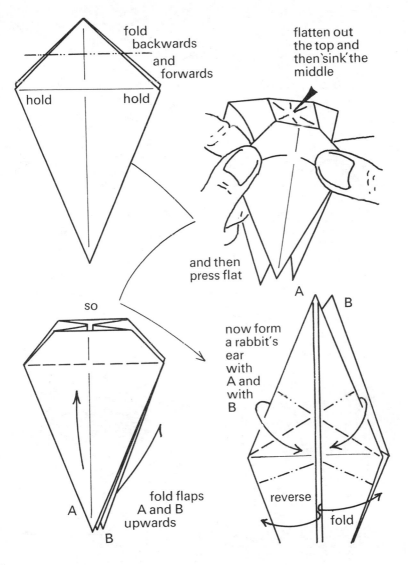

fold
backwards
and
forwards

hold   hold

flatten out
the top and
then 'sink' the
middle

and then
press flat

A

so

A   B

now form
a rabbit's
ear
with
A and
with
B

fold flaps
A and B
upwards

A

B

reverse

fold

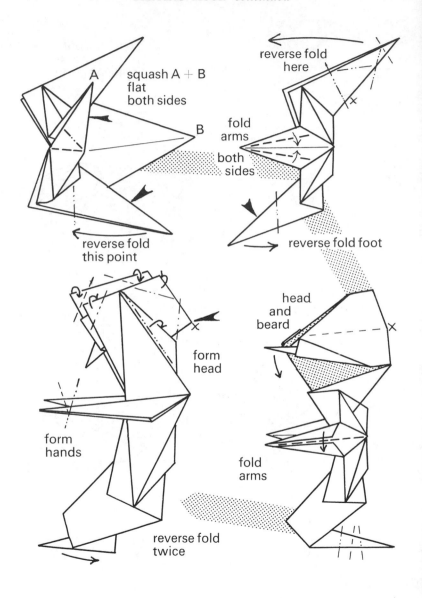

squash A + B
flat
both sides

reverse fold
this point

reverse fold
here

fold
arms
both
sides

reverse fold foot

form
head

form
hands

head
and
beard

reverse fold
twice

fold
arms

THE PRAYING MOOR
COMPLETED

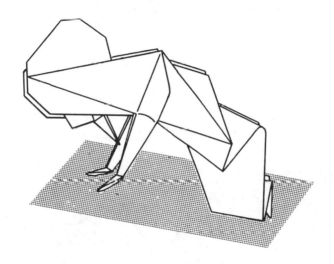

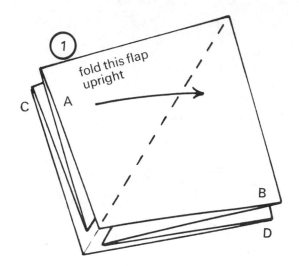

fold this flap upright

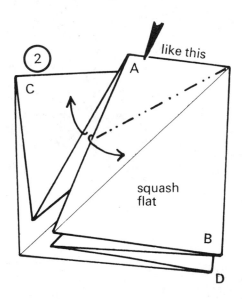

like this

squash flat

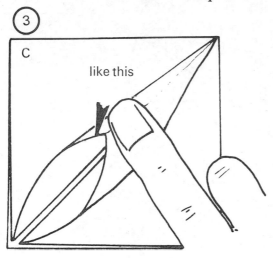

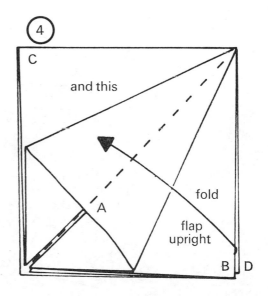

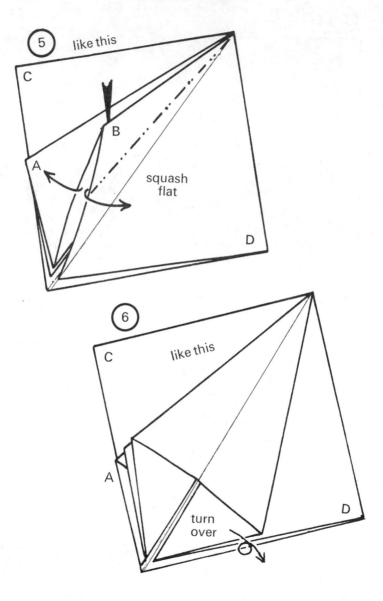

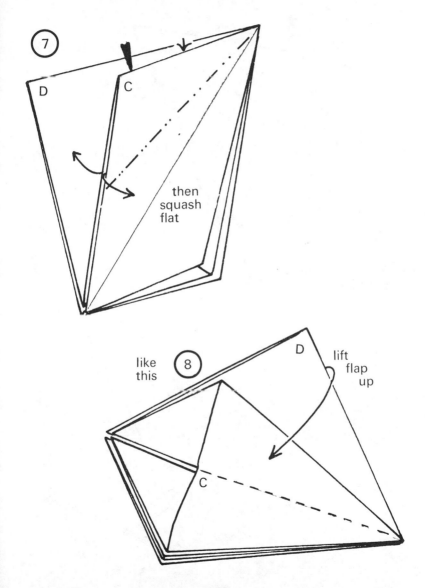

⑦ D C

then
squash
flat

like
this ⑧ D lift
flap
up

C

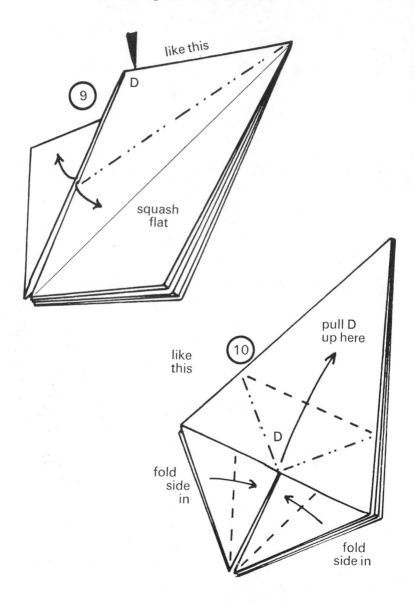

like this

D

⑨

squash
flat

like
this

⑩

pull D
up here

D

fold
side
in

fold
side in

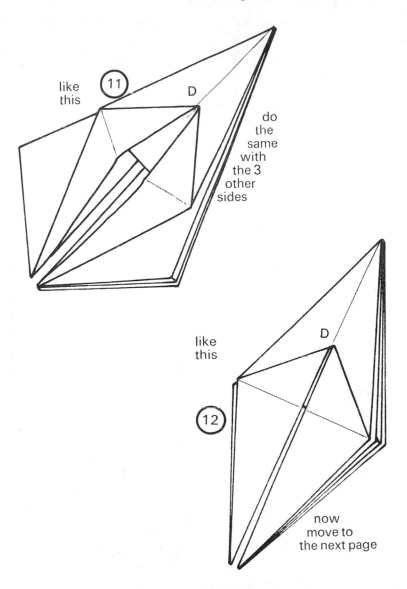

like
this

11

D

do
the
same
with
the 3
other
sides

like
this

D

12

now
move to
the next page

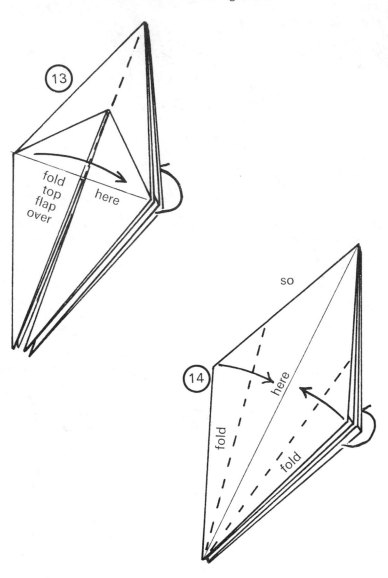

13 fold top flap over here

14 so fold here fold

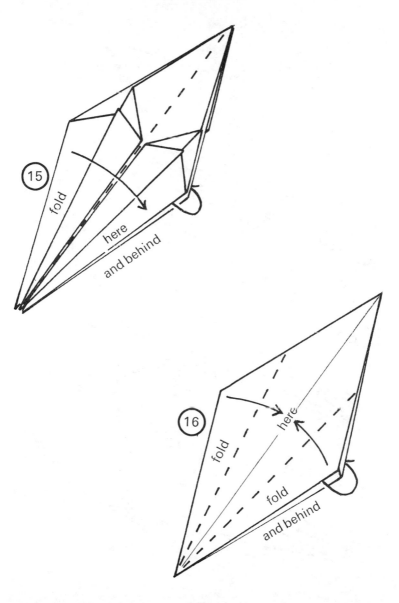

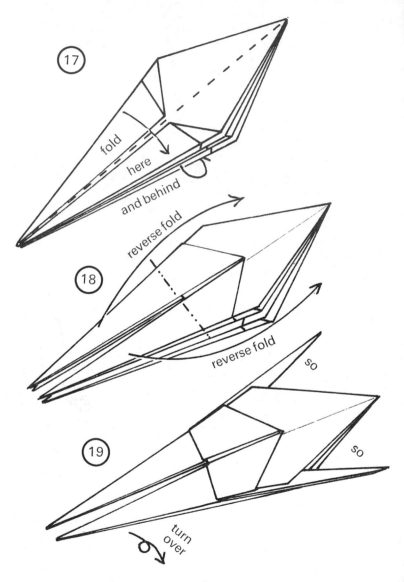

17 fold here and behind

18 reverse fold reverse fold

19 so so turn over

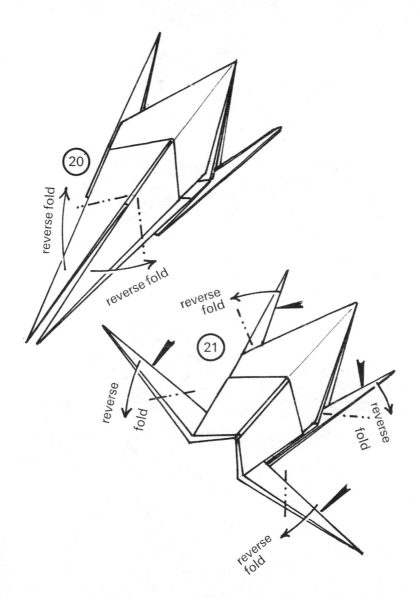

now reverse
fold
all tips

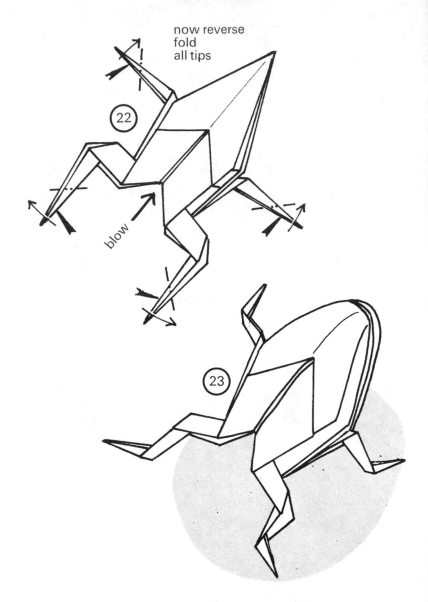

blow

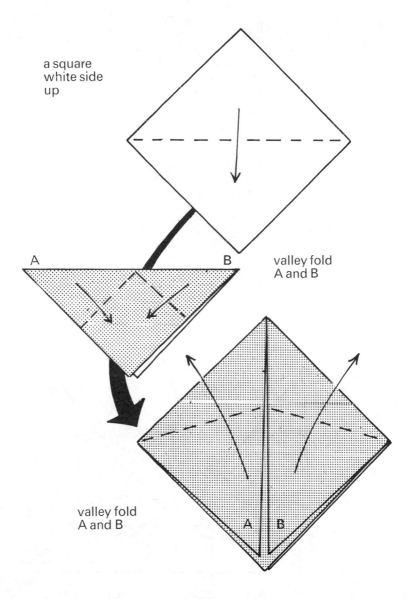

a square
white side
up

A   B   valley fold
A and B

valley fold
A and B

A   B

III

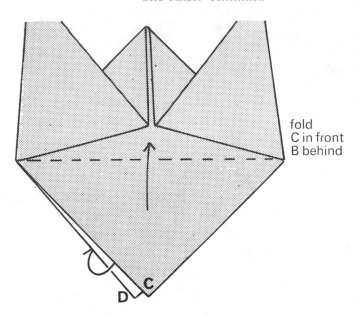

fold
C in front
B behind

C
rabbits' ear

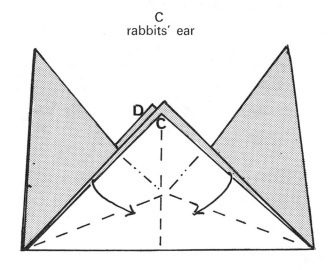

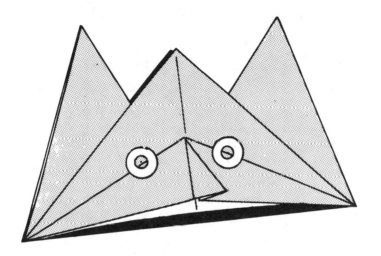

make eyes with gummed eyelets

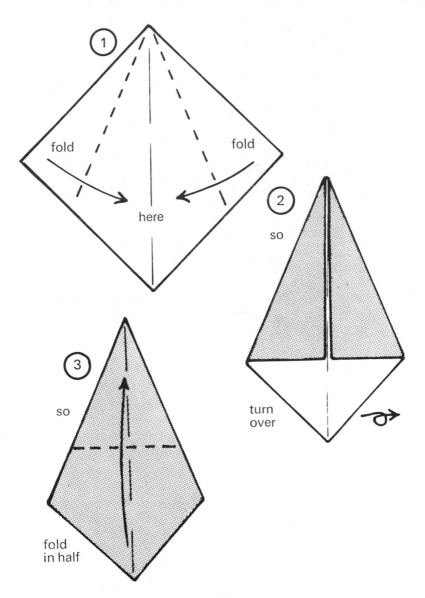

①

fold

fold

here

②

so

turn
over

③

so

fold
in half

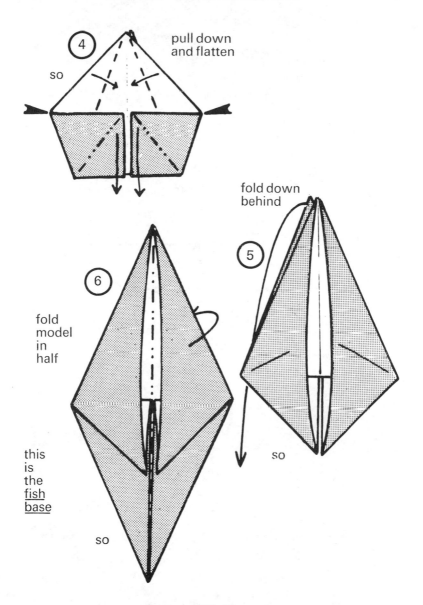

④ so
pull down
and flatten

⑤
fold down
behind

so

⑥
fold
model
in
half

this
is
the
fish
base

so

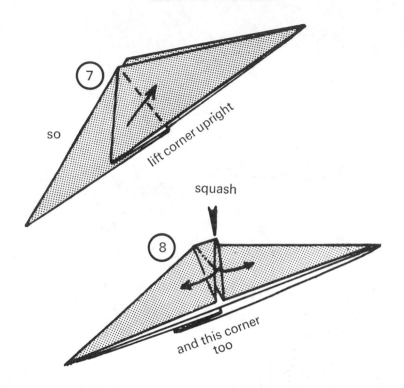

7 so

lift corner upright

squash

8 and this corner too

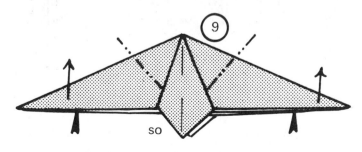

reverse fold both points

9 so

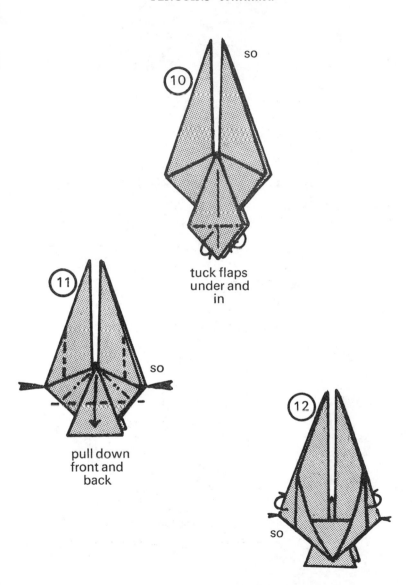

10 so

tuck flaps
under and
in

11 so

pull down
front and
back

12 so

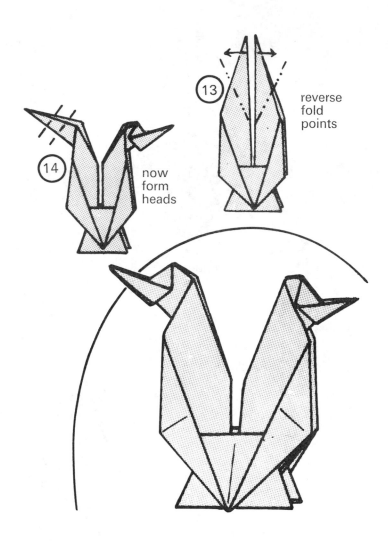

reverse
fold
points

now
form
heads

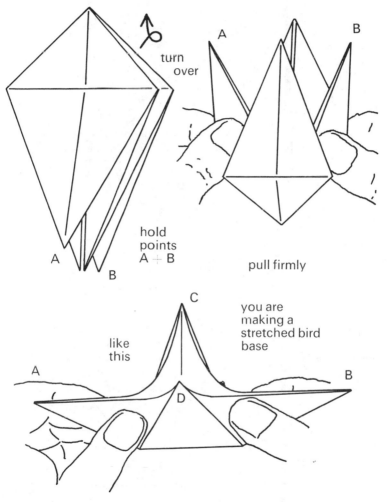

turn over

hold
points
A + B

pull firmly

C

you are
making a
stretched bird
base

like
this

A

B

D

bring C + D together press flat

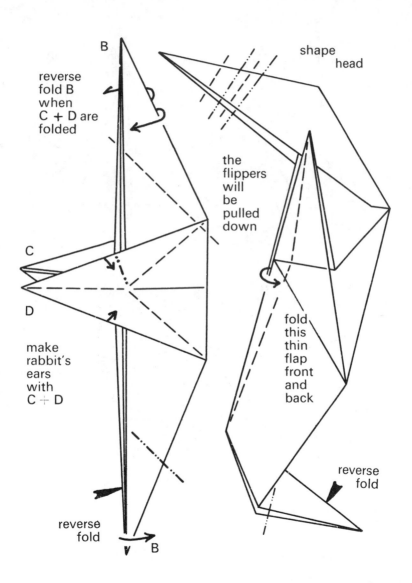

B

reverse
fold B
when
C + D are
folded

shape
head

the
flippers
will
be
pulled
down

C

D

make
rabbit's
ears
with
C ÷ D

fold
this
thin
flap
front
and
back

reverse
fold

reverse
fold

B

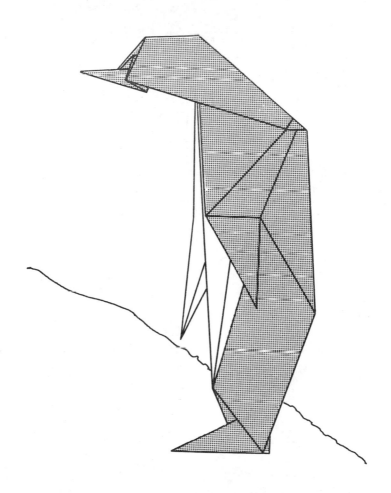

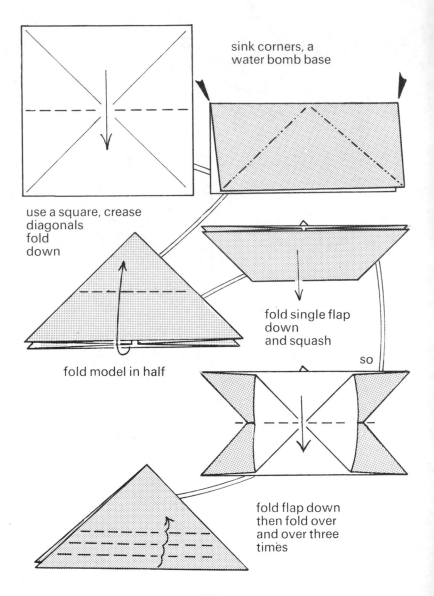

sink corners, a
water bomb base

use a square, crease
diagonals
fold
down

fold single flap
down
and squash

fold model in half

so

fold flap down
then fold over
and over three
times

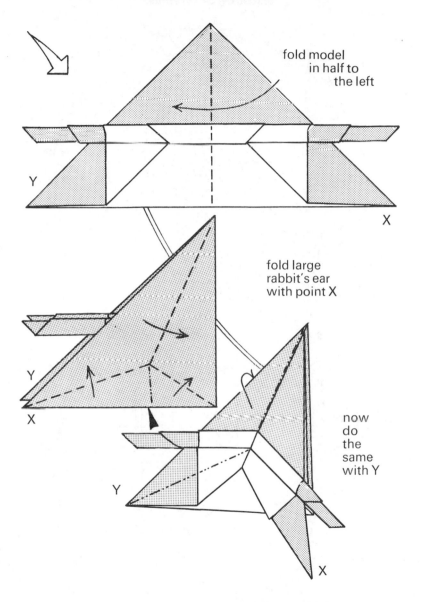

fold model
in half to
the left

Y

X

fold large
rabbit's ear
with point X

Y

X

now
do
the
same
with Y

Y

X

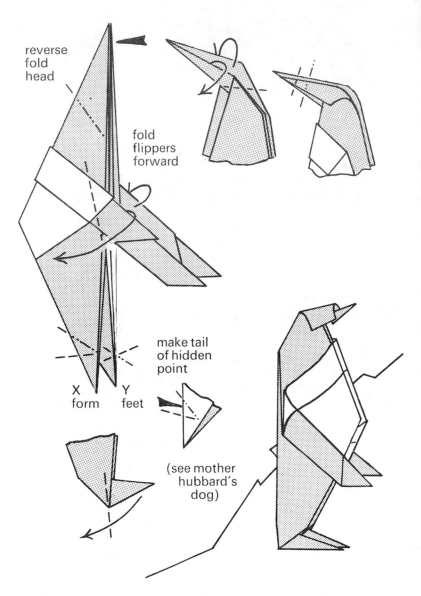

reverse
fold
head

fold
flippers
forward

make tail
of hidden
point

X   Y
form   feet

(see mother
hubbard's
dog)

RABBIT *Michael P. Guy, Birmingham, England*

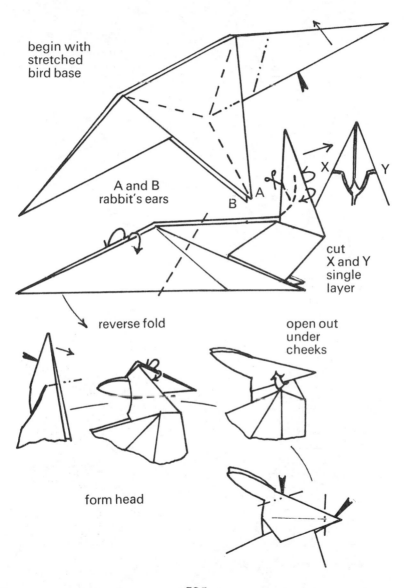

begin with
stretched
bird base

A and B
rabbit's ears

B A

X

Y

cut
X and Y
single
layer

reverse fold

open out
under
cheeks

form head

RABBIT *Using stretched Bird Base (see Penguin I)*

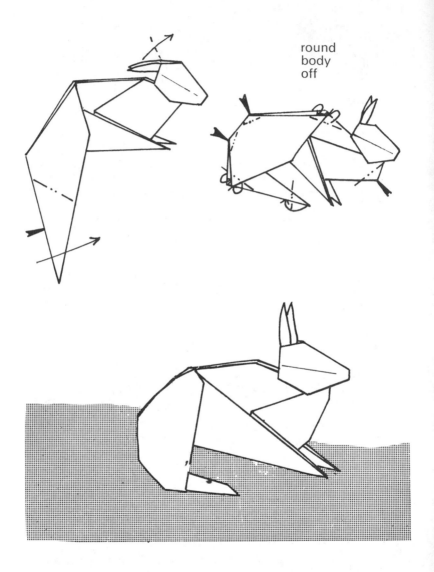

round
body

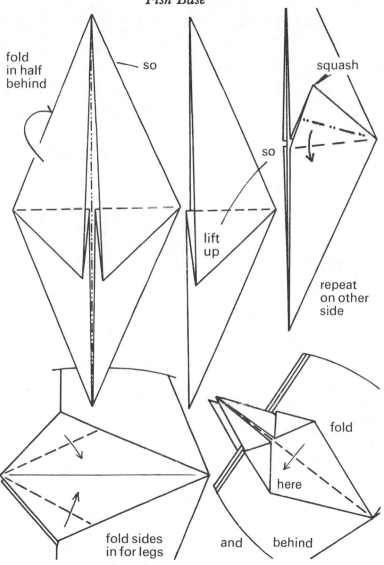

fold
in half
behind

so

squash

so

lift
up

repeat
on other
side

fold

here

fold sides
in for legs

and

behind

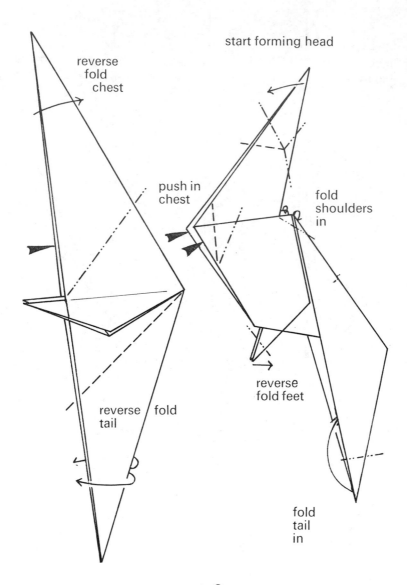

start forming head

reverse
fold
chest

push in
chest

fold
shoulders
in

reverse / fold
tail

reverse
fold feet

fold
tail
in

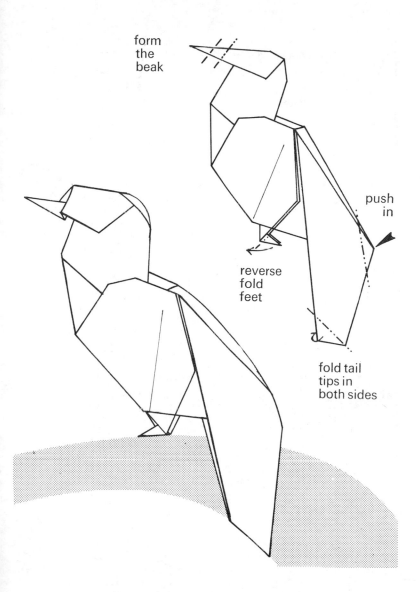

form
the
beak

push
in

reverse
fold
feet

fold tail
tips in
both sides

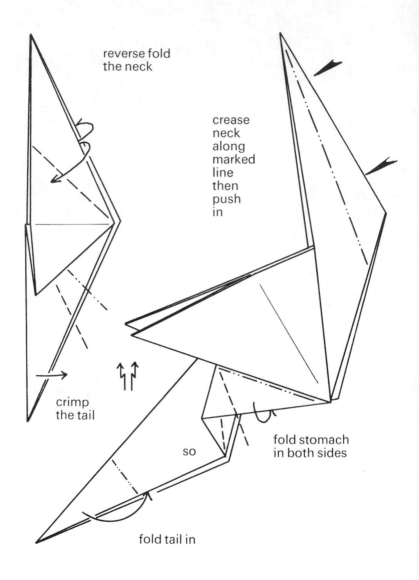

reverse fold
the neck

crease
neck
along
marked
line
then
push
in

crimp
the tail

so

fold stomach
in both sides

fold tail in

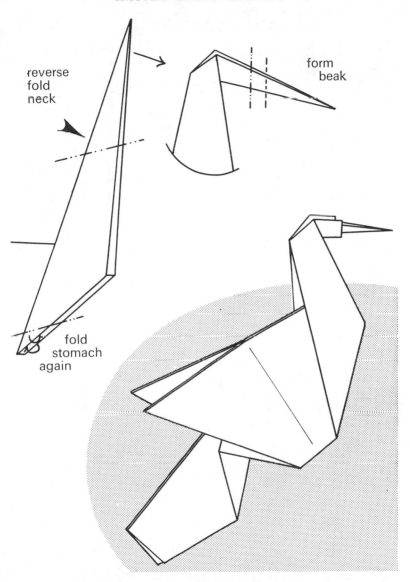

reverse
fold
neck

form
beak

fold
stomach
again

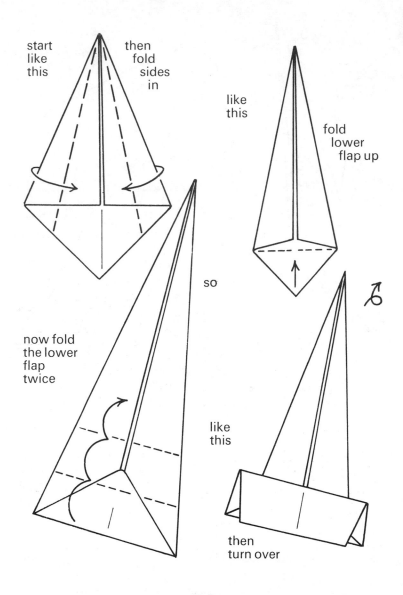

start
like
this

then
fold
sides
in

like
this

fold
lower
flap up

so

now fold
the lower
flap
twice

like
this

then
turn over

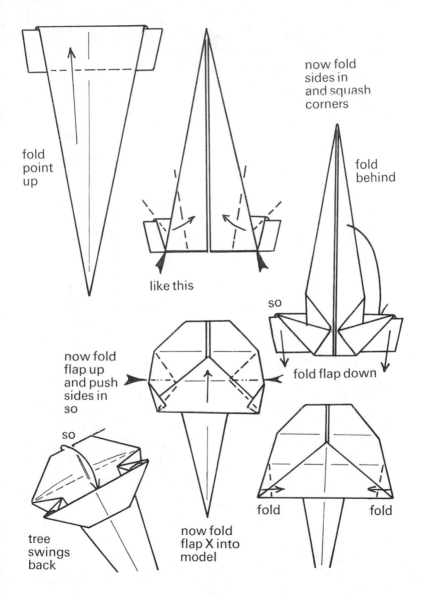

fold
point
up

now fold
sides in
and squash
corners

fold
behind

like this

so

now fold
flap up
and push
sides in
so

fold flap down

so

tree
swings
back

now fold
flap X into
model

fold   fold

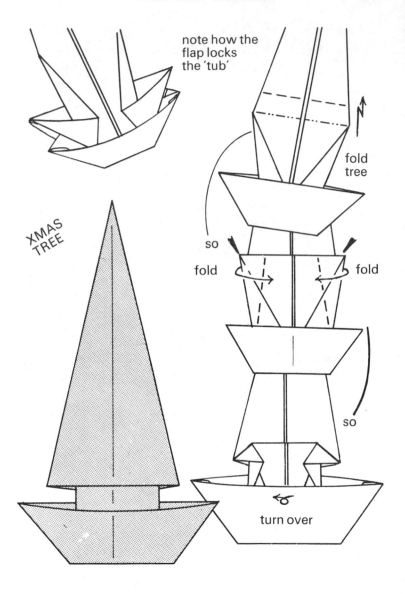

note how the
flap locks
the 'tub'

fold
tree

so

fold   fold

XMAS
TREE

so

turn over

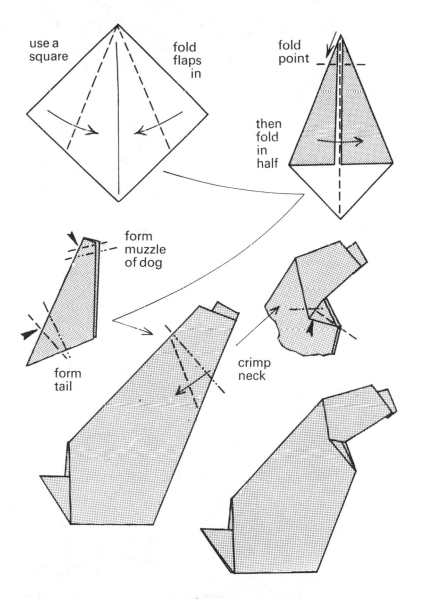

use a square

fold flaps in

fold point

then fold in half

form muzzle of dog

form tail

crimp neck

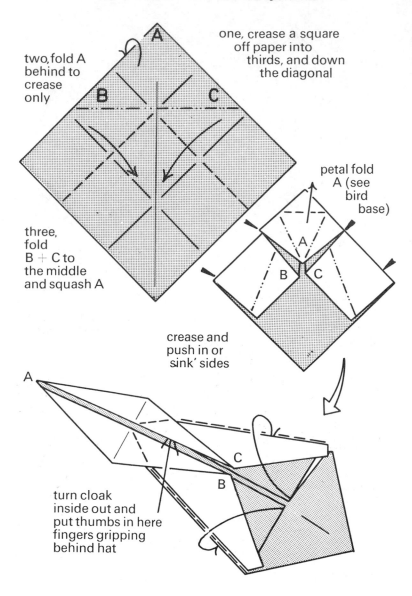

one, crease a square off paper into thirds, and down the diagonal

two, fold A behind to crease only

three, fold B + C to the middle and squash A

petal fold A (see bird base)

crease and push in or sink' sides

turn cloak inside out and put thumbs in here fingers gripping behind hat

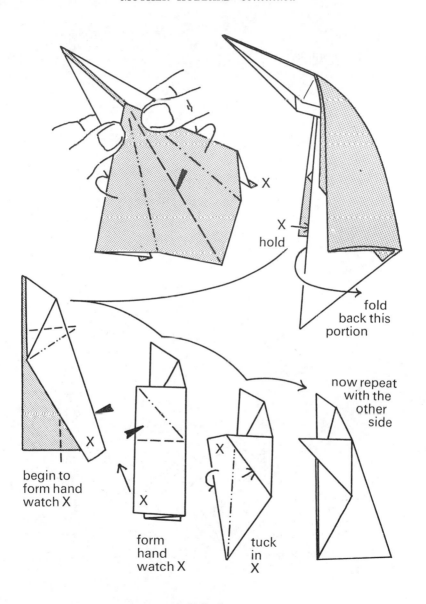

X

X
hold

fold
back this
portion

now repeat
with the
other
side

X

begin to
form hand
watch X

X

X

form
hand
watch X

X

tuck
in
X

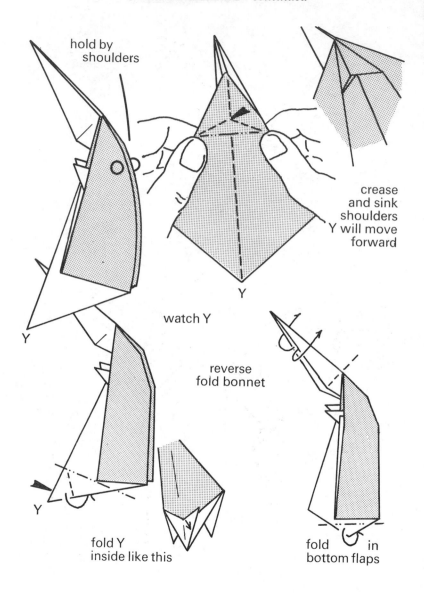

hold by
shoulders

crease
and sink
shoulders
Y will move
forward

Y

watch Y

reverse
fold bonnet

Y

fold Y
inside like this

fold   in
bottom flaps

bonnet
reversed

reverse
fold tip of
bonnet

(mother
hubbard's
dog explained
elsewhere)

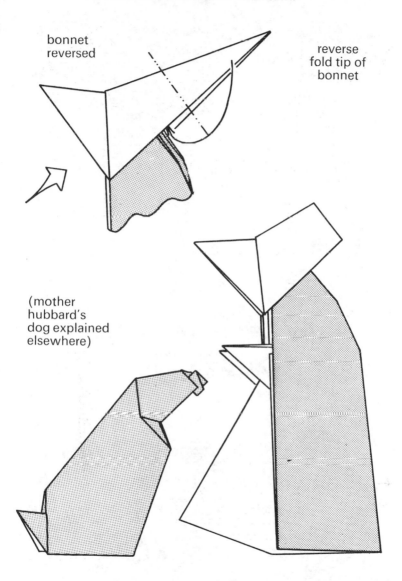

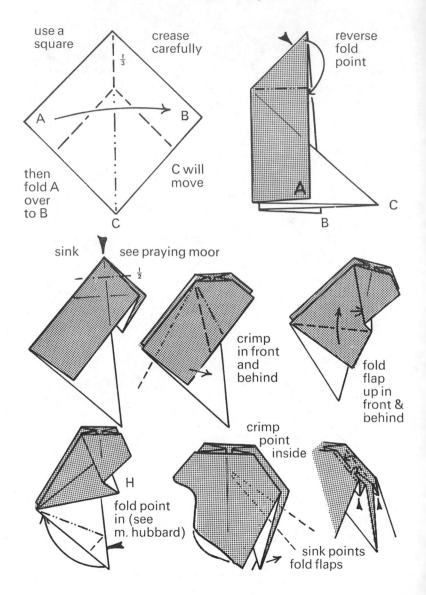

use a
square

crease
carefully

⅓

A   B

then
fold A
over
to B

C will
move

C

reverse
fold
point

A

C

B

sink   see praying moor

½

crimp
in front
and
behind

fold
flap
up in
front &
behind

H

fold point
in (see
m. hubbard)

crimp
point
inside

sink points
fold flaps

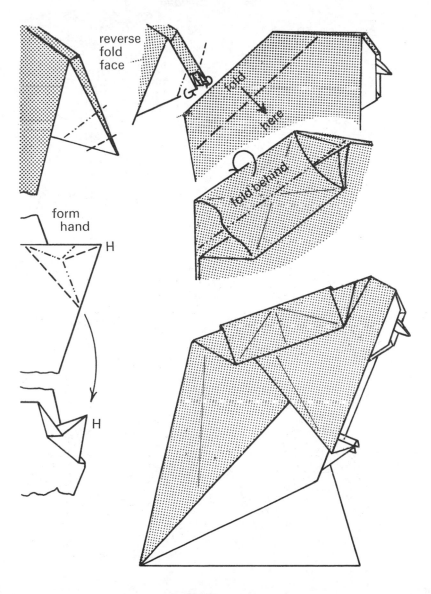

reverse
fold
face

fold

here

fold behind

form
hand

H

H

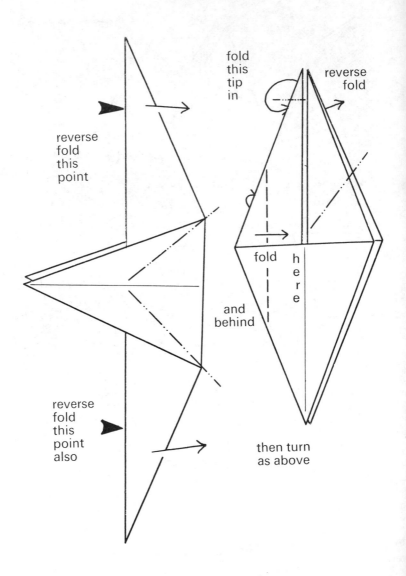

reverse
fold
this
point

fold
this
tip
in

reverse
fold

fold   h
              e
              r
              e

and
behind

reverse
fold
this
point
also

then turn
as above

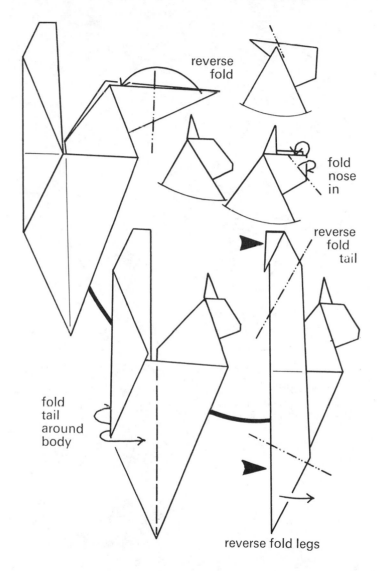

reverse
fold

fold
nose
in

reverse
fold
tail

fold
tail
around
body

reverse fold legs

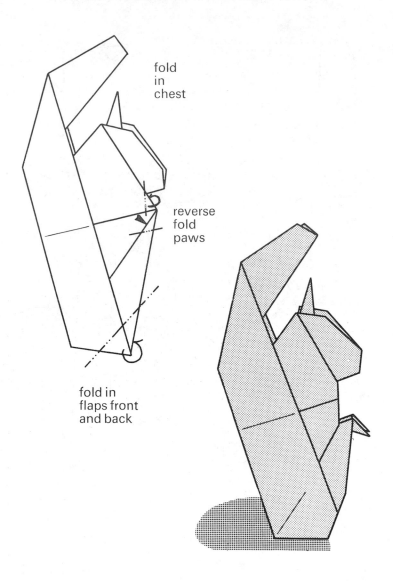

fold
in
chest

reverse
fold
paws

fold in
flaps front
and back

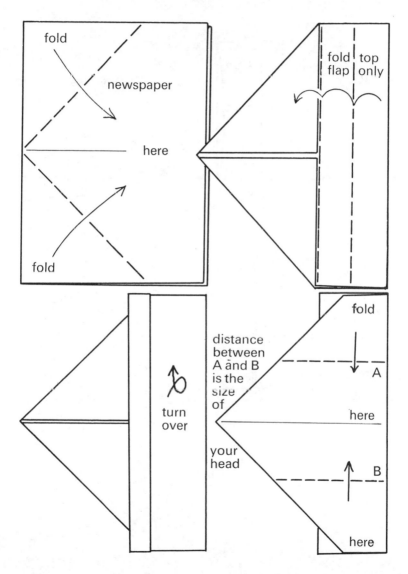

fold

newspaper

here

fold

fold top
flap only

distance
between
A and B
is the
size
of

turn
over

your
head

fold

A

here

B

here

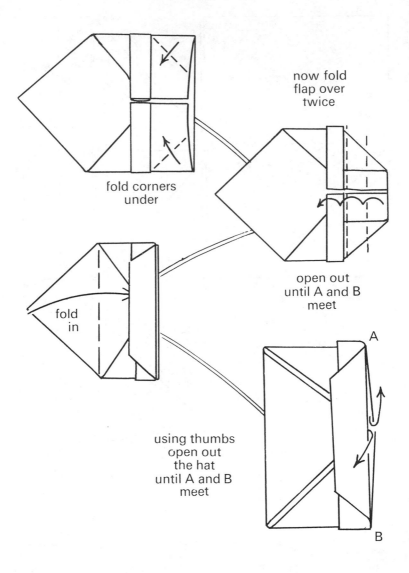

now fold
flap over
twice

fold corners
under

open out
until A and B
meet

fold
in

A

using thumbs
open out
the hat
until A and B
meet

B

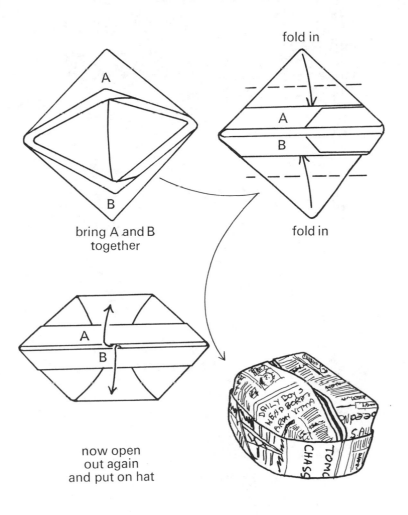

fold in

A

B

bring A and B
together

fold in

A

B

fold in

A

B

now open
out again
and put on hat

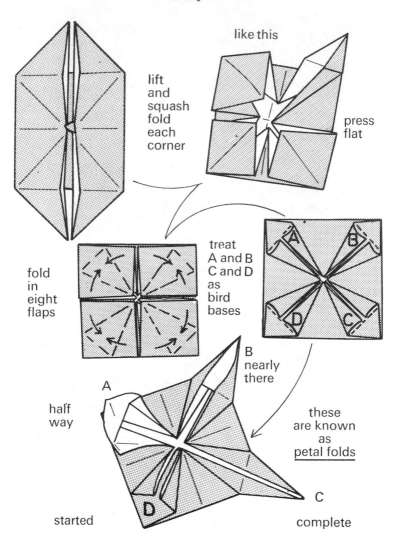

like this

lift
and
squash
fold
each
corner

press
flat

fold
in
eight
flaps

treat
A and B
C and D
as
bird
bases

A

B

B
nearly
there

half
way

A

these
are known
as
petal folds

D

C

started

complete

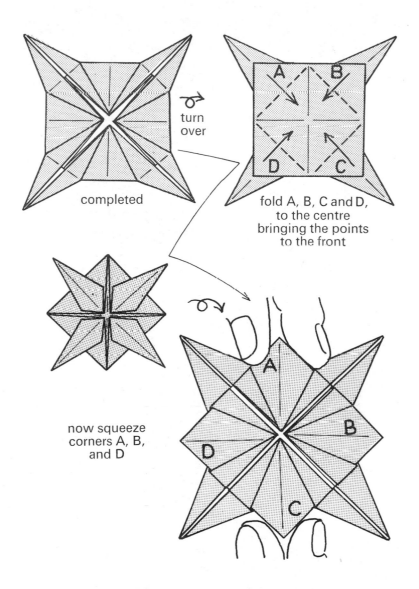

turn
over

completed

fold A, B, C and D,
to the centre
bringing the points
to the front

now squeeze
corners A, B,
and D

149

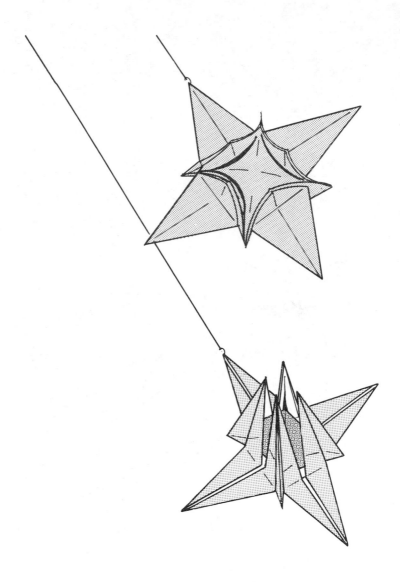

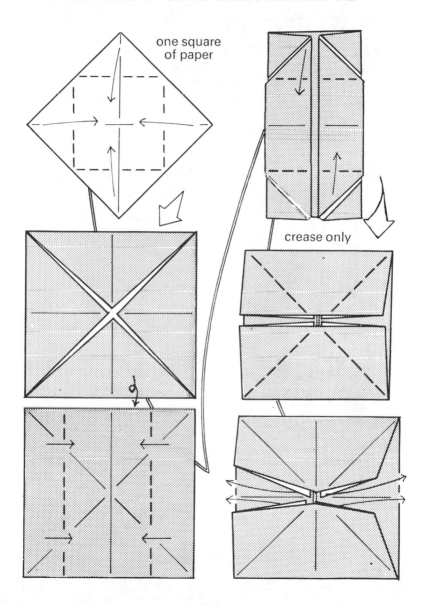

one square
of paper

crease only

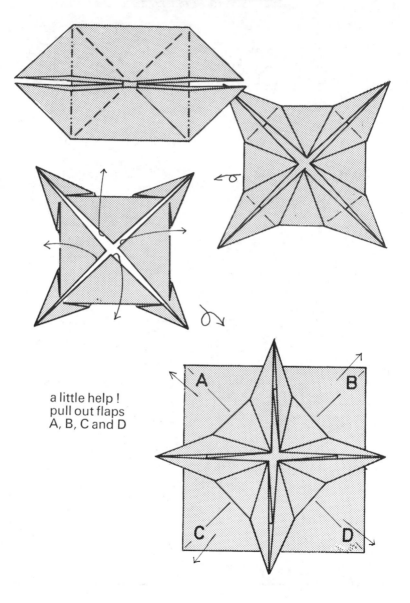

a little help !
pull out flaps
A, B, C and D

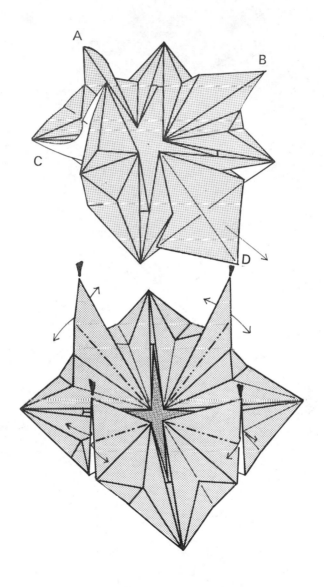

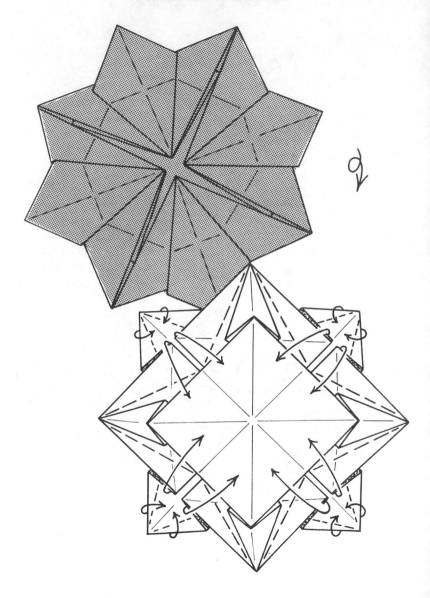

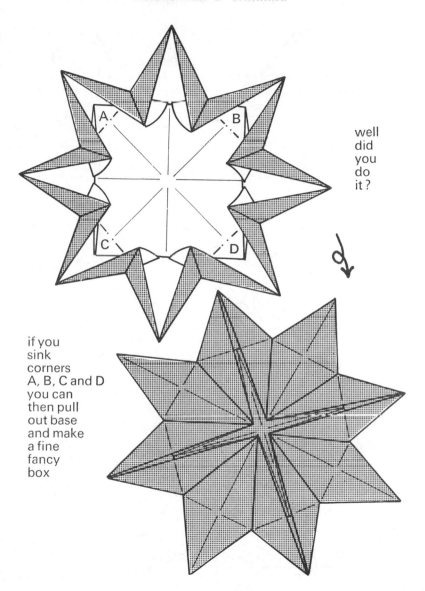

well
did
you
do
it ?

if you
sink
corners
A, B, C and D
you can
then pull
out base
and make
a fine
fancy
box

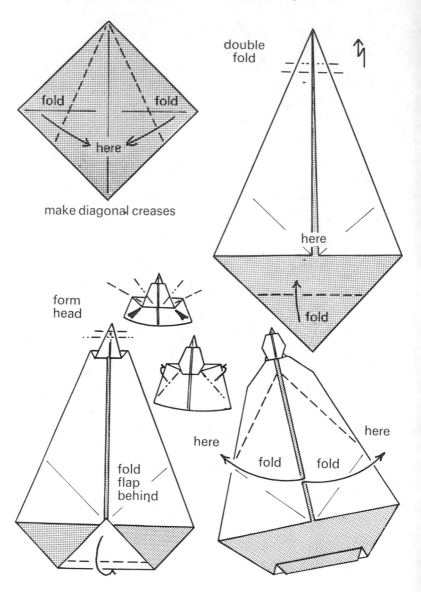

make diagonal creases

fold   fold

here

double
fold

here

fold

form
head

fold
flap
behind

here

fold   fold

here

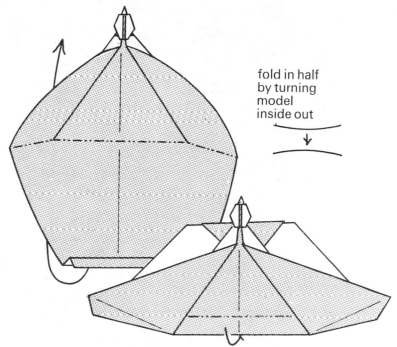

fold in half
by turning
model
inside out

fold along marked line only

when you fold flaps,
A and B will move upwards

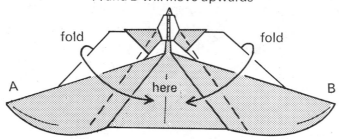

fold

fold

A

B

here

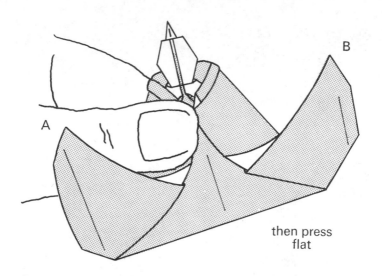

A

B

then press
flat

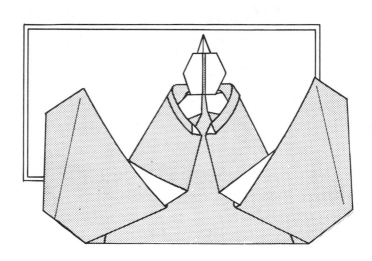

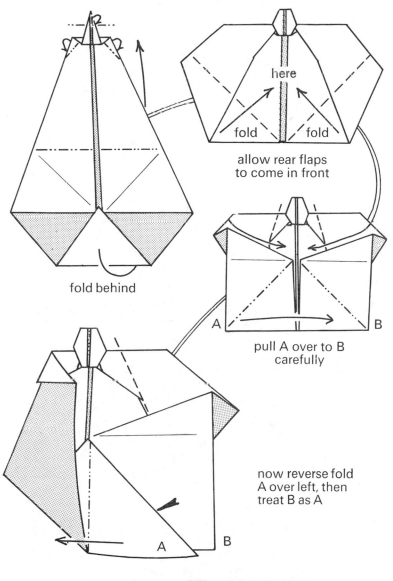

here

fold   fold

allow rear flaps
to come in front

fold behind

A   B

pull A over to B
carefully

now reverse fold
A over left, then
treat B as A

A   B

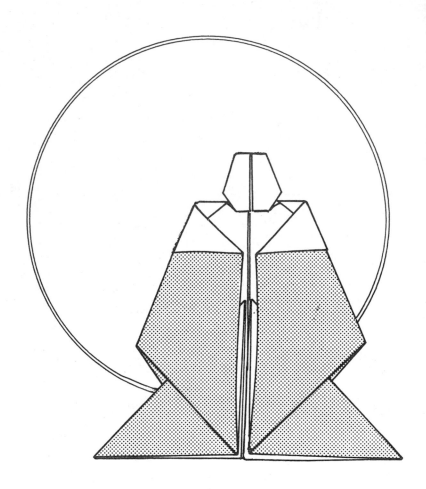

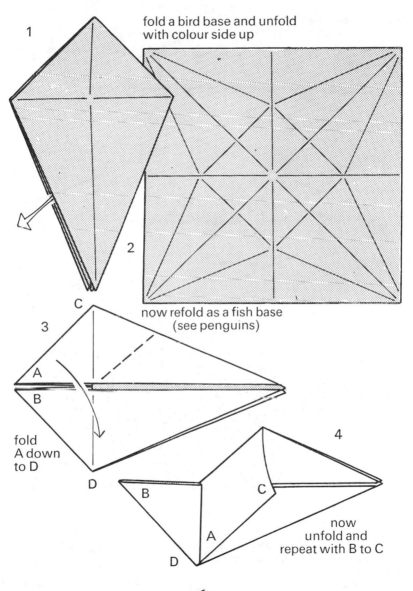

1

fold a bird base and unfold
with colour side up

2

now refold as a fish base
(see penguins)

3

C

A

B

fold
A down
to D

D

4

B

C

A

D

now
unfold and
repeat with B to C

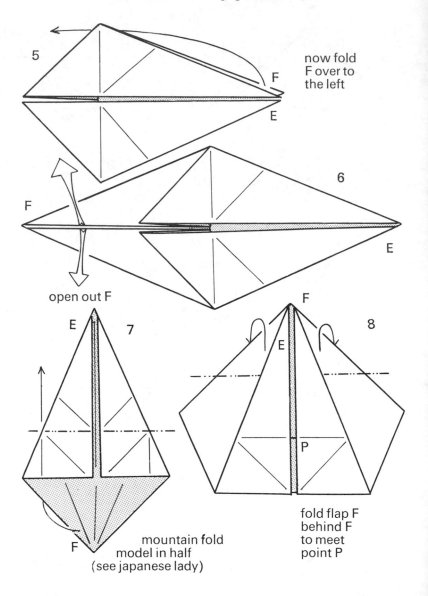

5

now fold
F over to
the left

F

E

F

6

E

open out F

E   7

mountain fold
model in half
(see japanese lady)

F

F   8

E

P

fold flap F
behind F
to meet
point P

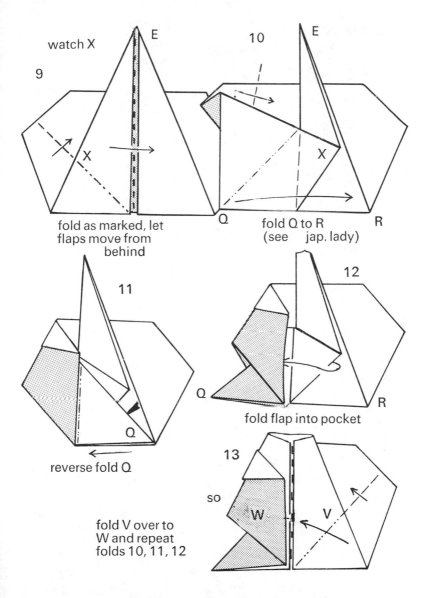

watch X

9

E

fold as marked, let
flaps move from
behind

10

E

X

Q   R

fold Q to R
(see   jap. lady)

11

Q

reverse fold Q

12

Q

R

fold flap into pocket

13

so

W   V

fold V over to
W and repeat
folds 10, 11, 12

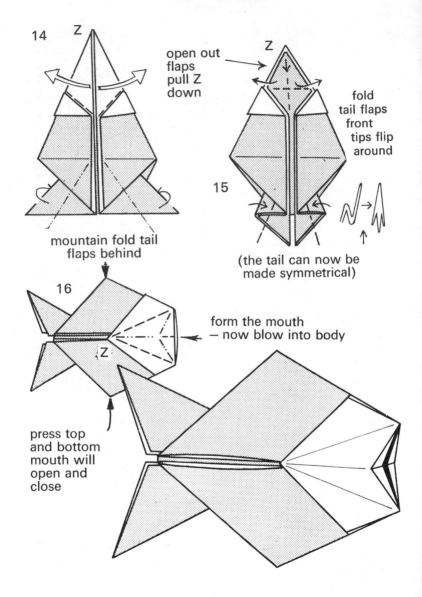

14

Z

open out
flaps
pull Z
down

Z

fold
tail flaps
front
tips flip
around

15

mountain fold tail
flaps behind

(the tail can now be
made symmetrical)

16

form the mouth
— now blow into body

Z

press top
and bottom
mouth will
open and
close

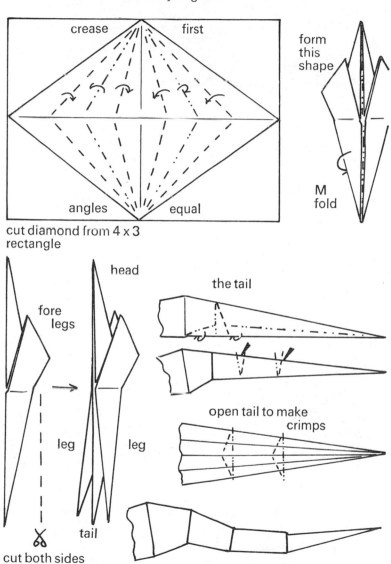

crease   first

angles   equal

cut diamond from 4 x 3 rectangle

form this shape

M fold

head

fore legs

leg   leg

tail

cut both sides of middle for legs

the tail

open tail to make crimps

the head and neck

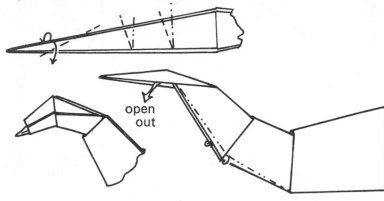

open out

back legs

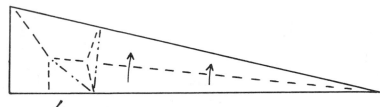

reverse fold

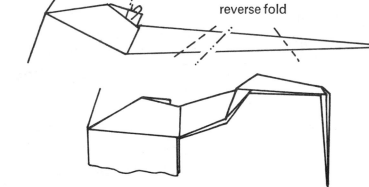

fore legs

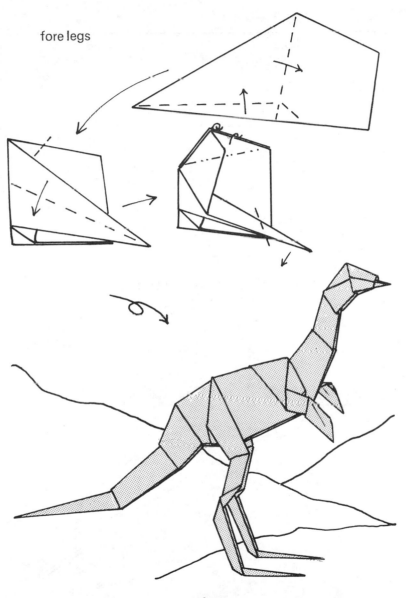

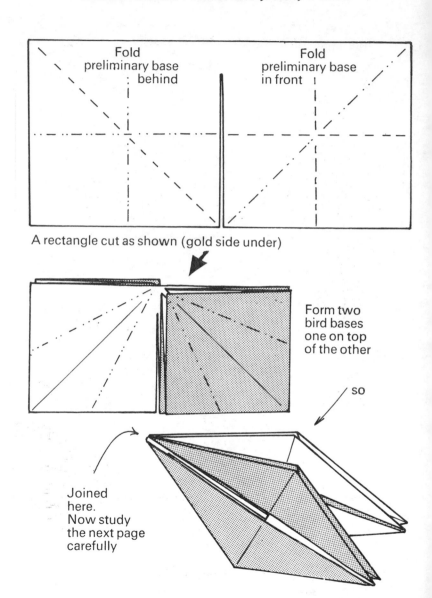

Fold
preliminary base
behind

Fold
preliminary base
in front

A rectangle cut as shown (gold side under)

Form two
bird bases
one on top
of the other

so

Joined
here.
Now study
the next page
carefully

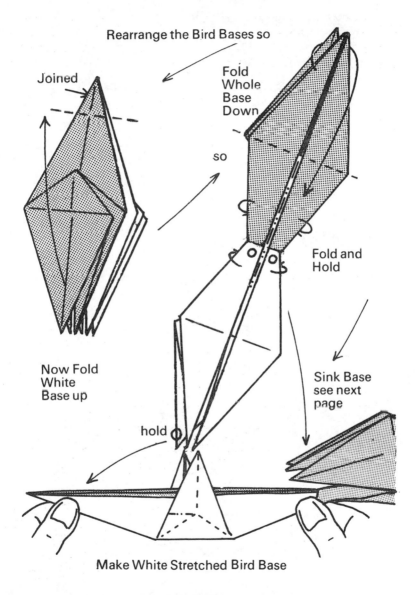

Rearrange the Bird Bases so

Joined

Fold
Whole
Base
Down

so

Fold and
Hold

Now Fold
White
Base up

Sink Base
see next
page

hold

Make White Stretched Bird Base

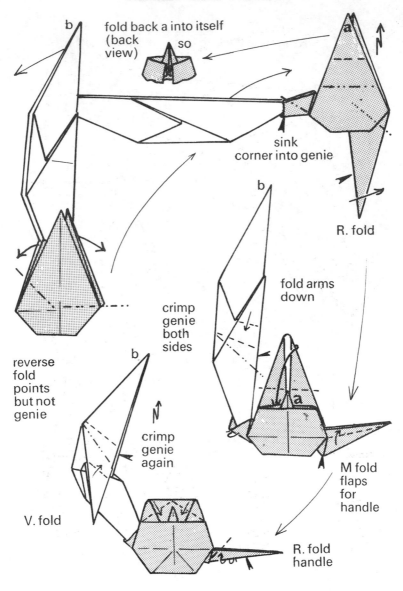

b

fold back a into itself
(back view) so

sink corner into genie

R. fold

fold arms down

crimp genie both sides

reverse fold points but not genie

crimp genie again

V. fold

M fold flaps for handle

R. fold handle

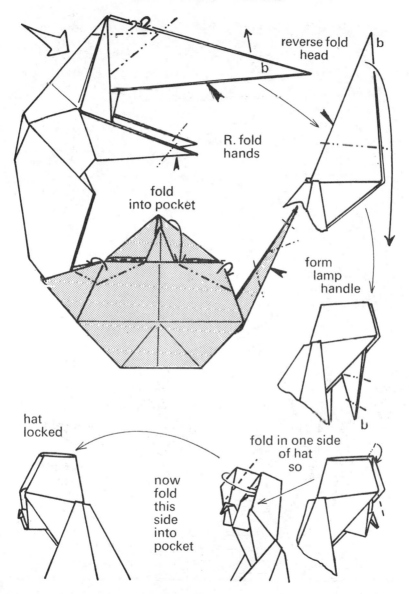

reverse fold
head

b

R. fold
hands

fold
into pocket

form
lamp
handle

b

hat
locked

now
fold
this
side
into
pocket

fold in one side
of hat
so

b

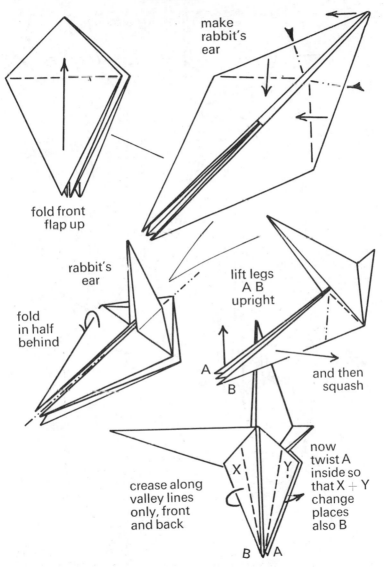

make rabbit's ear

fold front flap up

rabbit's ear

fold in half behind

lift legs A B upright

A
B

and then squash

crease along valley lines only, front and back

X   Y

now twist A inside so that X + Y change places also B

B   A

OSTRICH *Complete with Rider*

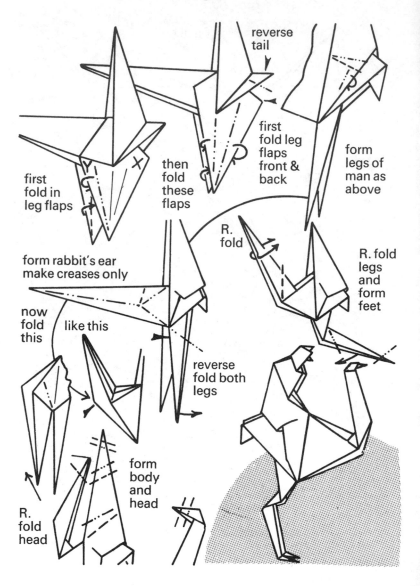

reverse
tail

first
fold leg
flaps
front &
back

form
legs of
man as
above

first
fold in
leg flaps

then
fold
these
flaps

R.
fold

R. fold
legs
and
form
feet

form rabbit's ear
make creases only

now
fold
this

like this

reverse
fold both
legs

R.
fold
head

form
body
and
head

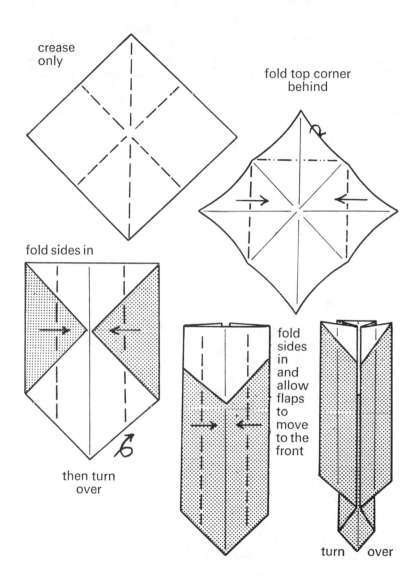

crease
only

fold top corner
behind

fold sides in

then turn
over

fold
sides
in
and
allow
flaps
to
move
to the
front

turn over

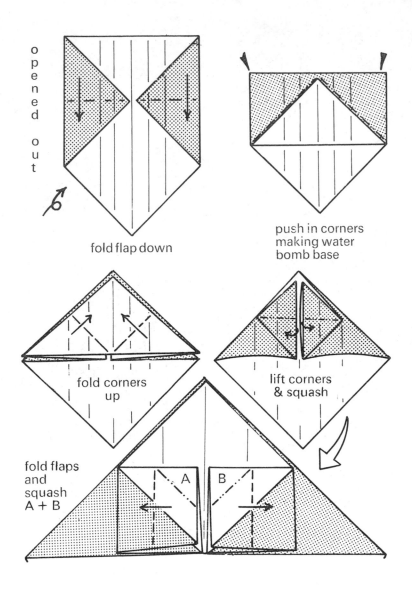

opened out

fold flap down

push in corners making water bomb base

fold corners up

lift corners & squash

fold flaps and squash A + B

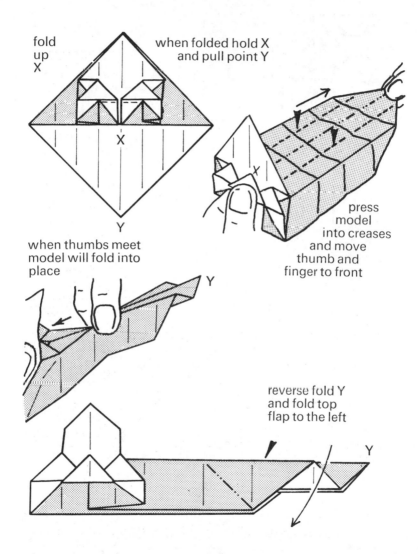

fold
up
X

when folded hold X
and pull point Y

X

Y

press
model
into creases
and move
thumb and
finger to front

when thumbs meet
model will fold into
place

Y

reverse fold Y
and fold top
flap to the left

Y

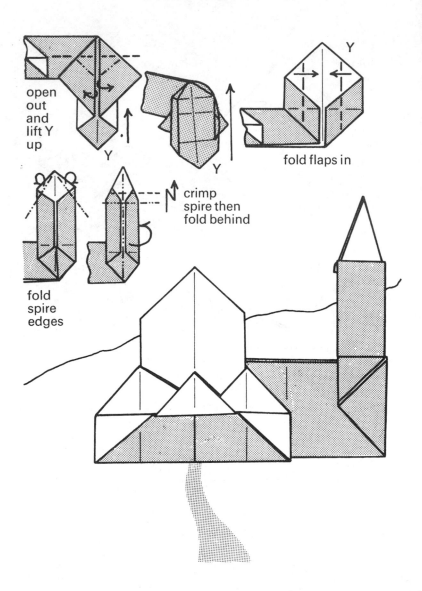

open
out
and
lift Y
up

fold flaps in

fold
spire
edges

crimp
spire then
fold behind

PINK ELEPHANT *Tim Ward and Trevor Hatchett London*

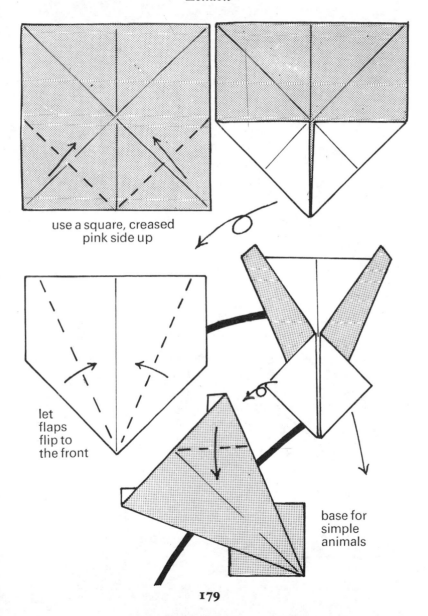

use a square, creased
pink side up

let
flaps
flip to
the front

base for
simple
animals

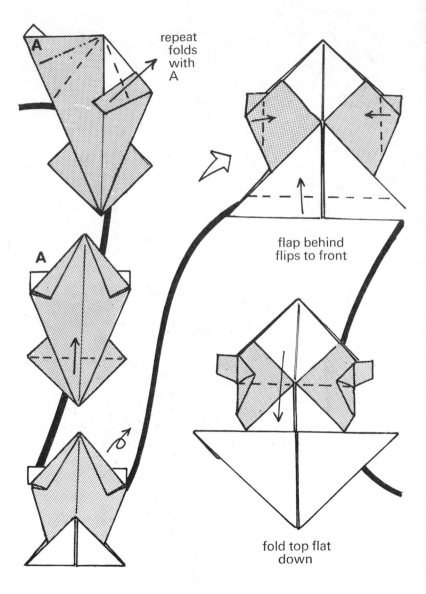

A

repeat
folds
with
A

A

flap behind
flips to front

fold top flat
down

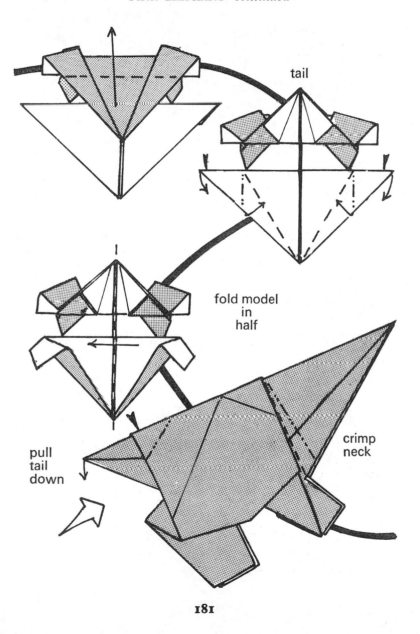

tail

fold model
in
half

crimp
neck

pull
tail
down

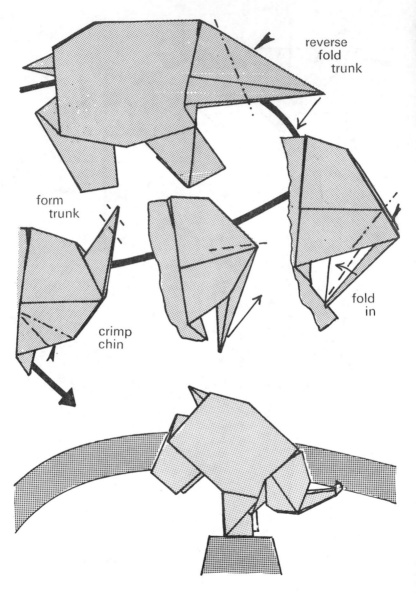

reverse
fold
trunk

form
trunk

crimp
chin

fold
in

SWANS *Tim Ward and Trevor Hatchett London*

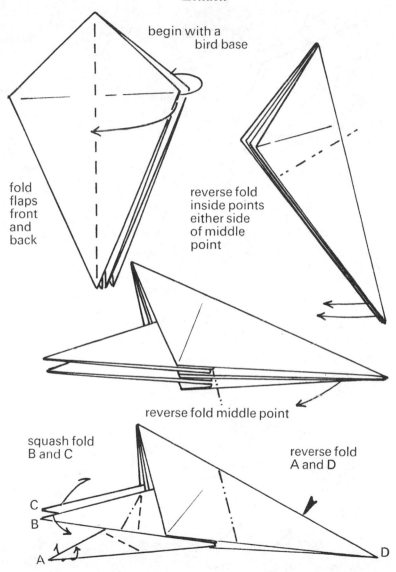

begin with a bird base

fold flaps front and back

reverse fold inside points either side of middle point

reverse fold middle point

squash fold B and C

reverse fold A and D

C
B
A
D

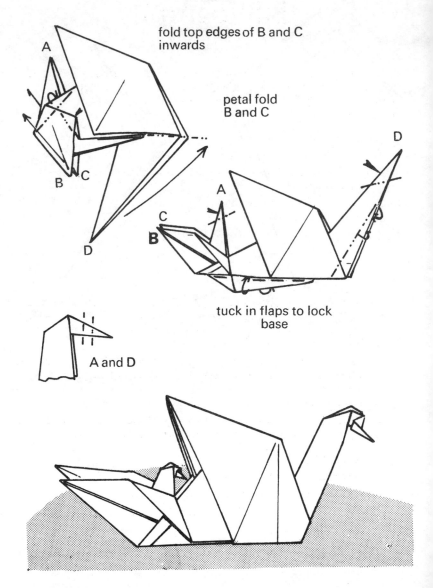

fold top edges of B and C inwards

petal fold
B and C

tuck in flaps to lock
base

A and D

Bibliography

by David Lister

Books about origami now number several hundreds, but many of these are designed for children. The following books include models of a wide range of difficulty and have been selected mainly for their interest for serious folders.

Harbin, Robert

Paper Magic (1956, this edition 1971), John Maxfield Ltd., London.

Secrets of Origami (1963), Oldborne Press Ltd., London. Later edition, Octopus Books, London.

Origami: A Step-by Step Guide (1974), Hamlyn Publicity Group Ltd., London.

Robert Harbin's books contain a wonderful selection of models and, taken in order of publication, his books are a valuable record of the development of origami from 1956 to 1977.

Randlett, Samuel

The Art of Origami (this edition 1963), Faber and Faber Ltd., London. This book contains many excellent traditional and modern models, as well as valuable articles on the history of origami and on teaching methods.

The Best of Origami (this edition 1964), Faber and Faber Ltd., London. This book shares a high reputation with *The Art of Origami*, not only for the excellence of the models, which complement those on Robert Harbin's books, but also for the high quality of the diagrams.

The Flapping Bird (1968–76), originally published as a periodical in 25 issues, now published as a book, Jay Marshall, Chicago, USA.

Kenneway, Eric

Simple Origami (1970), Dryad Press, Leicester.

Origami in Action (1972), Dryad Press, Leicester.

Folding Faces (1978), Paddington Press Ltd., London.
The development of the author's personal style to form portraits of well-known personalities. Includes a valuable short history of paper-folding.

Origami—Paper Folding for Fun (1980), Octopus, London.

Temko, Florence
Paper: Folded, Cut, Sculpted (1974), Collier Macmillan, London.
An interesting book containing simple origami in a setting of other papercrafts.

Gray, Alice and Kasahara, Kunihiko
The Magic of Origami (1977), Japan Publications Inc., Tokyo.
A collection of interesting models of moderate difficulty.

Kawai, Toyoaki
Origami (1970), Color Books, Osaka.
Creative Origami (1977), Color Books, Osaka.
Colourful books, printed in English, which can be found in UK and US bookshops.

Three classic works currently in print:

Murray, W. D. and Rigney, F. J.
Paper Folding for Beginners (1928; this edition 1960), Dover Publications, New York.

Campbell, Margaret
Paper Toy Making (1937; this edition 1975), Dover Publication, New York.

Soong, Maying
The Art of Chinese Paper Folding (1948; this edition 1964), World's Work Ltd., Surrey.
One of the few books on this subject from a Chinese author.

These were the best paper-folding books published in English before Robert Harbin's *Paper Magic*. They were the books from which Lillian Oppenheimer and Robert Harbin learnt much of their folding and are now principally interesting for their historical value.

Japanese Texts:

Japanese output is enormous, but most books are designed for children. Nevertheless, there are still many books of value to adults. The British Origami Society, or the Origami Center, New York, will advise on the best, and how to obtain them.

Japanese authors to look for include: Akira Yoshizawa, Kosho Uchiyama, Toshie Takahama, Toyoaki Kawai, Kunihiko Kasahara and Yoshihide Momotani.